AF249113

VOTES FOR WOMEN

VOTES FOR WOMEN

BY G. ALLEN FOSTER

Illustrated with photographs

CRITERION BOOKS - NEW YORK

The photographs in this book are
reproduced through the courtesy of:

Brown Brothers: pp. 26; 50; 76; 82; 94; 190; 196

New York Public Library: pp. title page; 24; 25; 31;
34; 36; 45; 48; 53; 60; 63; 65; 67; 70; 79;
99; 108; 124; 126; 153; 183

Underwood and Underwood News Photos, Inc.: pp.
153; 155; 161; 163; 164; 166; 170; 196; 200;
202; 203; 204

Wide World Photos, Inc.: p. 205

Acknowledgments

Hon. Norman H. Anderson, Attorney General of Missouri, Jefferson City, Mo.

Folkways Records & Service Corp., Album No. FH 5281, *Songs for Suffragettes*, 117 West 46th St., New York 36, N.Y.

Mrs. Alexander P. Guyol, League of Women Voters, Washington, D.C.

William P. Hilliker, Jr., Assistant to the Producer, Jules Power Productions.

Mrs. Margaret B. Morton, former member of the Smith College Marching Suffragettes, Plymouth, N.H.

Hon. Margaret Chase Smith, U.S. Senator from Maine, Senate Office Building, Washington, D.C.

TO
Margaret B. Morton
OF THE
SMITH COLLEGE
MILITANT MARCHING
SUFFRAGETTES

Contents

Illustrations

THE CONSTITUTION OF THE UNITED STATES
Article XIX

1. The right of citizens of the United States to vote shall not be denied or abridged by the United States or by any State on account of sex.

2. Congress shall have the power to enforce this article by appropriate legislation.

* * *

Oh, dear, what can the matter be?
Dear, dear, what can the matter be?
Oh, dear, what can the matter be?
Mothers are wanting to vote!

SUFFRAGETTE SONG OF THE 1890's

Foreword

On November 2, 1920, it is possible that your grandmother went to the polls for the first time and voted for either Warren G. Harding, Republican, or James M. Cox, Democrat, for President of the United States. There is a chance that she did not vote that November day, because after the long years of struggle for woman suffrage, there were still well-meaning ladies who believed in woman's rights, but who were not ready to concede that these rights included voting. It was still a man's world in 1920.

The Negro waited a hundred years for a federal law guaranteeing him the right to vote *everywhere,* although the Constitution has guaranteed him that right ever since the ratification of the Fourteenth Amendment. However, there are states where he has been voting since 1790, and free Negroes voted in each of the original thirteen states except Georgia.

But until August 26, 1920, when the Nineteenth Amendment was ratified, the word "sex" had never appeared in the Federal Constitution. This was the final victory in the battle for woman suffrage which had raged relentlessly since 1837.

While there was no Selma, Birmingham, or Philadelphia, Mississippi, in the woman suffrage movement, there were marches, sit-ins, rotten eggs and overripe tomatoes. Many men marched with the women, subjecting themselves to the derision of their male friends. Policemen broke up the marches. But just as Sheriff Jim Clark of Selma focused the eyes of the nation on Martin Luther King, assuring his victory, so the police billy clubs of New York and Washington helped to bring victory to the women.

Today, because they live longer, there are more women than men in the United States. Nevertheless, it is impossible to estimate the influence of the women's votes, because they can't be identified. But no political party underestimates the "woman vote." What politician, even as late as World War I, could have predicted that in 1965, a hundred women would be members of the Republican and Democratic National Committees; that in the Coolidge administration there would be a woman Assistant Attorney General; that in 1932, Nellie Taylor Ross would be Governor of Wyoming; that there would be a woman Secretary of Labor in FDR's Cabinet; and that in 1964, Senator Margaret Chase Smith of Maine would be the first serious woman candidate for the Republican presidential nomination?

1 *The Curse of Eve*

The scene was a courtroom in the early 1830's and old
Judge Buller was presiding. The prosecution had just
closed its case which was now ready for the jury. The
county solicitor (attorney) asked the jury to find the
defendant guilty of "unreasonably beating his wife." In
charging the jury, Judge Buller said: "Without undertaking
to define exactly what a reasonable instrument is, I hold,
gentlemen of the jury, that a stick no bigger than my thumb
comes clearly within that description." The next day, a
committee of women called on the judge to see the thick-
ness of his thumb.

Emily Collins, who founded the first woman's rights
society at South Bristol, New York, in 1848, recounted: "I
remember in my own neighborhood a Methodist class-
leader and exhorter, esteemed a worthy citizen, who every
few weeks gave his wife a horsewhipping. He said it was
necessary in order to keep her in subjection "because she
scolded so much." Of this not uncommon practice Emily
Collins observed: "Now this wife, surrounded by six or

seven little children, whom she must dress, feed and attend to day and night, was obliged to spin and weave cloth for all the garments of the family. She had to milk the cows, make butter and cheese, do all the cooking, washing, sewing and mending for the family, and, with the pains of maternity forced on her every eighteen months, was whipped by her pious husband, *'Because she scolded.'* " Yes, in those days a man had a legal right to beat his wife — reasonably.

In the first half of the nineteenth century, women possessed no legal rights whatsoever. A married woman's earnings belonged to her husband. He had sole control of the children while he lived. In his will he could direct that, upon his death, the children be taken away from their mother and given to a stranger. When the husband died, unless he had willed his home to his wife, she could remain in it only forty days without paying rent. A woman could not make a contract, nor could she make a will unless she left everything to her husband. In a New Hampshire law-book of 1843, entitled *Justice and Sheriff,* there is a special section for "Any infant, married woman, or insane person. . . ."

Just as slavery was justified biblically by the Southern clergy before the War Between the States, and for some years after, religion was on the side of the American male throughout most of the nineteenth century. Ministers quoted the Old Testament: "Thy desire shall be to thy husband, and he shall rule over thee." Or they cited St. Paul's warning: "Let your women keep silence in the churches for it is not permitted them to speak. . . . I suffer not a woman to teach, nor to usurp authority over man, but to be in silence."

But even more oppressive to women than either the laws

or the churches was public opinion, both male and female. Women were barred from the professions and most occupations. It was unladylike to work behind a counter in a store. There was no clerical work for women. A woman could work only as a domestic, or slave fourteen hours a day in a New England textile mill where her health was ruined in a short time.

The woman was further enslaved by her inability to get an education. In 1840, no college admitted women. There were no secondary schools for teen-age girls. It was the public consensus that a woman should be literate only to the point that she could read the Bible to her children and keep the home accounts. Education beyond this level would spoil her for being a dutiful housewife, it was said. True, there were some very literate women both in the United States and Europe, and some who had the audacity to write for publication. But of such women, the distinguished British author, Charles Lamb (1775-1834) said, "The woman who lets herself be known as an author, invites disrespect."

But it had not always been thus in America. When the Declaration of Independence was duly signed and read publicly on July 4, 1776, and the Liberty Bell had been rung, women were eligible to vote in New Jersey, some parts of Virginia and Maryland, and Massachusetts.

In Massachusetts, under the Old Province Charter, women voted from 1691 to 1780 for all elective offices. With the adoption of the first Massachusetts constitution, women and free Negroes voted for all offices except governor, executive council, and legislature from 1780 to 1785. The franchise was taken away from women with the ratification of the Federal Constitution.

But before the Declaration of Independence had been completed, Abigail Adams, the wife of John, who was working on the early drafts, wrote to him, "I long to hear you have declared an independence, and, by the way, in the new code of laws you will have to make, I desire that you would remember the ladies, and be more favorable to them than your ancestors. . . . If particular care and attention are not paid to the ladies, we are determined to *foment rebellion,* and will not hold ourselves bound to obey any laws in which we have no voice or representation!"

John Adams didn't "remember the ladies," and Abigail didn't "foment rebellion." One against George III was enough, but the State of New Jersey saw it differently. Hard upon the heels of the Declaration, the New Jersey constitution conferred the elective franchise upon "all inhabitants of this colony full of age, who have in cash or property, fifty pounds [approximately $200]." In spite of this, perhaps an oversight when the constitution was drafted, there is no evidence that women exercised their franchise. But in 1790, a Quaker legislator, belonging to that sect in which women had always had equal rights with men, introduced a constitutional amendment inserting "he or she" into the voting eligibility section. The amendment passed, but still no women voted—their husbands wouldn't have approved. This argument was heard again in 1920.

Then came a surprise to New Jersey males. In 1797, there was a state election and a hot contest in Elizabethtown, Essex County. National political parties had not developed at this time, but in New Jersey there were two embryo parties: the Federal-Republicans and the Federal-Aristocrats. John Condit was running for the legislature on the former and William Crane was the Federal-Artistocrat candidate. As the men, unaccompanied by their wives, filed past the ballot box, it was obvious that the vote would be extremely close. But late in the day, just as the polls were about to close, in marched candidate Crane followed by seventy Elizabethtown housewives. The registrars were stunned and could hardly believe their eyes. A woman had never been seen in a polling place before. But Crane read to them from the state constitution, and the women voted. Crane lost anyway.

After that election of 1797, Elizabethtown husbands probably ordered their wives to stay at home and mind their own business on election days, but their orders were not long to be heeded. The presidential election of 1800 was bound to be close, and it was generally conceded that the electoral vote of one state could throw the Presidency to either Jefferson or Burr. In fact, the election later proved to be an electoral tie, and was decided for the first time in the House of Representatives. On that Election Day, the women of New Jersey, black and white, turned out in droves. The men shook their heads. Then in the 1802 state election, the New Jersey women of both races polled enough votes to decide several contests for the legislature. This was *just too much,* and the subsequent legislature amended the constitution, excluding New Jersey women from voting.

But in spite of the puritanical clergy, the county judges, and the man in the street, there were women who had the courage to ignore this vast barrier to woman's freedom and social advancement. In 1830 or thereabouts, a woman named Mary Lyon was going about Massachusetts to raise funds for a female educational institution which she was to call Mount Holyoke Seminary, now a distinguished college for women.

But neither Mary Lyon nor the women of New Jersey were alone in their quest for woman's rights. As early as 1790, an Englishwoman, Mary Wollstonecraft, had published *The Vindication of the Rights of Women,* which was widely read on both sides of the Atlantic and furiously attacked by the clergy. In 1797, Frances Wright, Scottish by birth, was lecturing on woman's rights in America; and in France, following the Revolution of 1789, the women were vainly demanding the ballot.

In spite of Charles Lamb's warning to women writers that they would "invite disrespect" if published, Anna Franklin published the first Rhode Island newspaper in 1732, her two daughters setting type; and in New York City, the *Weekly Journal* was edited by Mrs. Peter Zenger after her husband's death.

Washington had its first woman newspaper publisher in 1829, Anne Royall of *The Huntress,* a weekly. Mrs. Royall specialized in interviewing visiting notables and blackmailing people who didn't subscribe to her paper. According to eccentric E. Ben Perley:Moore, an able contemporary Washington news correspondent, "Mrs. Royall's tongue at last became so unendurable that she was formally indicted by the Grand Jury as a common scold. The Circuit Court jury found her guilty, and under the laws of the District of Columbia, she should have been ducked in a pond. But her counsel begged His Honor Judge Cranch to weigh the matter and not be the first to introduce a ducking stool. The plea prevailed, and she was let off with a fine."

Throughout the fight for woman suffrage, from the days of the French Revolution to Nellie Taylor Ross's election as Governor of Wyoming, there was a combination of movements and developments which were interlocked with the feminist cause. Prior to the Civil War, they were *slavery and liquor.*

Women joined the antislavery and temperance movements for several reasons, principally because they were needed, but also because they could speak out at meetings without being labeled as brash. In the 1840's, antislavery societies were unpopular even in New England. They were so hard put for membership that the Abolition leader, William Lloyd Garrison, was glad to admit women to his ranks, and here the women who were to become the leaders of the woman's rights movement received their training, learning to speak effectively and to handle hecklers with dignity. Further, a long-range purpose inspired these women to join ranks with Garrison. If women could participate in fighting to end Negro slavery, why couldn't they at the same time struggle for their own freedom?

Throughout most of the nineteenth century, there had been periodic attacks by the clergy and social reformers on the use of alcoholic beverages and the liquor industry. During the 1840's and 50's, an enormous amount of liquor was consumed by the American male. The lighter wines and beers were not being produced in any considerable quantity, and the American drinking man had his choice of rye or bourbon whiskey, New England rum or "white mule" (corn whiskey). The laborer left too much of his week's pay at the corner saloon. It was common to see senators and congressmen intoxicated on the floors of their chambers. Men were maimed and killed in drunken brawls.

To stem this tide of national boozing, temperance societies were formed, but with most American males, they were far less popular than the antislavery groups. Thus, here again the women were needed, and here they had a real stake. A drunken husband, knowing that he had a legal right to beat his wife, would very likely do so if she scolded him for coming home on Saturday night with "one too many." If the woman was working in a factory, her alcoholic husband could take her wages to buy liquor, and the

Lucretia Coffin Mott, born in 1793, was one of
America's earliest crusaders for women's rights.

wife couldn't stop him. Yes, the housewife had a real
interest in the temperance movement, and here, too, she
was welcomed, and encouraged to use her brains in the
techniques of a crusade. As in the antislavery movement,
we find in the temperance movement the names of the
woman leaders who would make suffrage headlines in the
next fifty years.

The first of these names was Lucretia Coffin Mott.

As her partner in launching the movement, Mrs. Mott chose brilliant Elizabeth Cady Stanton.

Lucretia was born on the Island of Nantucket in 1793. She was educated in the Boston public schools in 1806, and later transferred to the Quaker Academy in Poughkeepsie, New York. After marrying James Mott, also a Quaker, in 1811, she remained for a few years in Poughkeepsie, teaching school. Lucretia Mott developed an extraordinary talent for public speaking at meetings of the Society of Friends (Quakers). As the woman's rights movement developed, many of its leaders, male and female, were Quakers. They came to it naturally because in the Friends' meetinghouses there was no discrimination against women. Having earned a reputation as a platform speaker, Lucretia Mott toured the East, lecturing on temperance, international amity, and woman's rights. She pleaded for woman's property rights, but, at that time, did not yet mention voting.

A younger woman, through an unforeseeable incident, was soon to become the partner of Lucretia Mott in the feminist crusade. Elizabeth Cady Stanton was born in 1815. As a young girl, she played with dolls in her father's law office in Johnstown, New York. There she heard the bitter complaints of women who came to her father's office seeking advice on their legal rights, and discovering they had none. In her teens, Elizabeth won a prize in Greek, and was certainly eminently fitted for any institution of higher learning, but no college would admit her. Bitterly disappointed, she studied by herself, and took an active part in the antislavery movement. And now comes the incident that touched off the fire that burned until August, 1920.

Great Britain was considerably more advanced than the United States in the antislavery movement, and would free her slaves long before Lincoln's Emancipation Proclamation. In 1840, the British Anti-Slavery Society sent out a call to a World Anti-Slavery Convention to be held in London, opening on June 12. Naturally, the United States was expected to send a delegation.

When the convention call was received by the Abolitionists in America, it was noted that there was no mention of the delegates' sex. Thus, since women had done outstanding work in the movement, among the delegates elected were Lucretia Mott and Elizabeth Stanton. Up to the time of their election, they had not known each other. Aboard the ship, the forty-seven-year-old Lucretia Mott and Elizabeth Stanton, aged twenty-five, became inseparable friends.

On the morning of June 12, after a long, rough voyage, they appeared at Freemason's Hall in London where the convention was to sit. At eleven o'clock, the convention was called to order by the British antislavery leader, Thomas Clarkson. However, Clarkson was in poor health, and he asked the great American orator and Abolitionist, Wendell Phillips (sometimes called "the unagitated agitator"), to take over the gavel. Phillips proposed a motion: "That a committee of five be appointed to prepare a correct list of the members of the convention, with instructions to include in such list *all persons* bearing credentials from any anti-slavery society."

Now a carefully rehearsed scene was enacted. A group of New England clergymen, who believed in freedom for the Negro, but not for women, and who had come on an earlier ship, had successfully stirred up the wrath of many British delegates by passing the word that the United States was sending two of its most dangerous women. Their plot was successful, for no sooner had Wendell Phillips finished reading his motion, than the attack was launched. Mrs. Stanton later recalled: "The Reverend J. Burnet, an Englishman, made a most touching appeal to the American ladies to conform to English prejudices and customs, so far as to withdraw their credentials, as it never occurred to the British and Foreign Anti-Slavery Society that it was inviting women."

Then the American clergy "got into the act." The Rev. Henry Grew, a delegate from Philadelphia, said: "The reception of women as a part of this convention would, in the view of many, be not only a violation of the customs of

England, but of the ordinance of Almighty God."

Next, the Rev. Eben Galusha of New York came in with the "one-two punch": "I commend to the consideration of our American female friends, who are so deeply interested in the subject, the example of your noble Queen Victoria, who by sanctioning her consort, His Royal Highness Prince Albert, in taking the chair on an occasion not dissimilar to this, showed her sense of propriety by putting her head foremost in an assembly of gentlemen, I have no objection to woman's being the neck to turn the head, but do not wish to see her assume the place of the head."

There was a vote, and Lucretia Mott and Elizabeth Stanton were evicted from the Anti-Slavery Convention. This act of injustice by the British and part of the American delegation accomplished for woman's rights what "Bull" Connor did for Martin Luther King over a hundred years later. But, of course, the ladies could not know this. When the two women left the convention hall, they were joined by William Lloyd Garrison and several other American delegates who refused to sit in a conclave which wouldn't recognize what women had done for Abolition in America.

During the remaining days of the London convention, Mrs. Mott and Miss Stanton went sightseeing and agreed to hold a woman's rights convention on their return to the United States. As Mrs. Stanton put it: "As the men to whom they had just listened had manifested their need of some education on the question." She concluded the chapter in her memoirs of the London convention: "The movement for woman suffrage, both in England and America, may be dated from this World's Anti-Slavery Convention."

Written in 1881, Elizabeth Stanton's assessment of the London incident was eighty per cent correct. But she and Lucretia Mott were unable to call a woman's rights convention immediately upon docking in Manhattan, and it would be ten years before they would accomplish their goal. The Mott-Stanton team was organization-minded, and properly so, but while they were trying to build an organization, a quiet, attractive young woman, an innate "loner," was planting the seeds of the Great Crusade.

2   *Lucy Stone: Pioneer*

Lucy Stone had the good fortune to be born in Massachusetts where wife-beating was illegal. As far back as the seventeenth century, Judge Sewall, who presided at the Salem witchcraft trials, pushed a bill through the state legislature which read: "Every married woman shall be free from bodily correction or stripes by her husband, unless it be in his own defense upon her assault."

Nine years after Abraham Lincoln's birth, Lucy Stone came into the world in 1818. As a grown woman, she was beautiful by modern standards, but in her day, her figure was considered too full to be ladylike.

Lucy's father, Francis Stone, was a veteran of the Revolution. Her childhood was spent on a farm in West Brookfield, Massachusetts. Upon learning the sex of her child, Mother Stone had said, "Oh, dear! I am so sorry she is a girl. A woman's life is so hard." But Lucy's childhood was happy. She had a pet sheep which jumped rope with her, and her dog, Bogue, helped herd the cattle. Studying the many different rocks on the farm, she learned elementary geology without a book. For spending money she

Beautiful Lucy Stone, a fearless agitator for women's rights was married to Henry Blackwell, but refused to be known by her husband's name.

sewed leather work shoes for four cents a pair. Lucy learned the psalm tunes of the Congregational Church by singing them with her brother while helping him fill the kitchen woodbox. Then she learned to read the psalms. There was no school which admitted girls in West Brookfield.

Lucy later credited her iron nerve to having been brought up on a farm where snakes, wildcats, bears, and lynxes were ever present. In her long years of campaigning for woman's rights, she faced mobs, overripe fruit, and rotten eggs "with never a quickened heartbeat," as she recalled in her old age. Elizabeth Stanton could inspire suffrage conventions, Victoria Woodhull could provide glamour, and Carrie Chapman Catt could organize marches. But it was Lucy Stone who pioneered the battle for woman's rights with calm fearlessness. She was never an orator, but she spoke in simple, deliberate sentences whenever and wherever the opportunity presented itself. She never lost her temper or her determination.

Even as a girl, Lucy Stone was infuriated over the status of wives in American society. The daily Bible reading by her father after supper eventually reached: "Thy desire shall be to thy husband, and he shall rule over thee." Lucy was convinced that this was not what God intended, and she vowed to learn Greek in order to find out what the Bible said in the original. But where could a girl learn Greek in 1832?

Lucy's Christian faith received another jolt when the family Bible reading came to Ephesians 5:22-24: "Wives be in subjection to your husbands, as unto the Lord. For the husband is head of the wife, as Christ also is head of the church. . . . But as the church is subject to Christ, so let wives also be subject to their husbands." Lucy silently noted that this was a quotation from St. Paul, not Christ.

By the time Lucy Stone was twelve, she was one of the few girls admitted to the local public school. However, she was needed at home because of her mother's failing health, so Lucy's school attendance was sporadic. Then one night there was an event which had never before occurred in West Brookfield, nor, for that matter, in any New England community. A *woman* spoke at the meetinghouse! Hadn't Paul said, "Let your women keep silence in the churches"? And in the old New England towns, the same building served as the town hall and the Congregational Church.

The woman was Mary Lyon, and she was speaking to raise money for her new Mount Holyoke Seminary. It is doubtful that Mary Lyon raised any money for Mount Holyoke in West Brookfield that night. New Englanders were generally favorable to education — for boys, that is. A girl might be more useful in the home if she finished eighth grade, but of what possible use was a secondary education for females? When Lucy Stone left the Mary Lyon meeting, her mind was set. She was determined to become an educated woman, the equal of any educated man.

First, Lucy needed money. This she began to acquire by teaching the "winter term" at the school in Paxton, Massachusetts, for one dollar a week. In so doing she broke a precedent, the first of many she would break in her long life. Precedent dictated that women were not competent to teach the winter term, because the classes in all grades were filled with the larger boys who were released from farm work when the snow was deep. The last teacher of the Paxton winter term had been a young man who had resigned after being beaten and thrown out the window into a snow bank by the older boys. Men in Paxton predicted that Lucy Stone wouldn't last through the first morning

Higher education was for men only until Mary Lyon founded
Mt. Holyoke College in 1836.

recitation — but they didn't know Lucy. The older, more troublesome boys knew a desirable, well-built girl when they saw one, and Lucy had the specifications. There was not one spitball thrown during the entire term, and the woodbox by the stove was always full.

In 1837, Lucy Stone was inspired by two sisters who shocked male America, but who were the harbingers of the woman's rights movement to come. At the time, Lucy didn't know that she would usher it in. These two young ladies were the Grimké sisters, daughters of a wealthy, slave-owning family in North Carolina. They had left the Episcopal Church and joined the Quakers. Worse than that, in the eyes of their family and friends, they were spurning St. Paul's command, and had started out on a tour of lectures which were given in *churches* before *audiences of women*.

Their eloquence came to the attention of William Lloyd Garrison, who invited them to join his Anti-Slavery Society and lecture throughout the East.

Next, the Grimké sisters rocked the sacred chambers of the Massachusetts legislature by appearing at a House committee hearing to speak for an antislavery resolution which was under consideration. But now, Sarah Grimké alienated some of Garrison's most devoted followers by attacking, in his *New England Spectator,* the social and economic slavery of women. Several Congregational ministers resigned from the Anti-Slavery Society because of Sarah Grimké's writings. Rights for blacks? Yes, they said. For women? No! And Lucy Stone read every word that Sarah Grimké wrote.

After teaching in several schools, Lucy accumulated enough money to enter Mount Holyoke Seminary. Mary Lyon, the founder and director, had a strong personal interest in foreign missions, and she encouraged her students

The great anti-slavery man, William Lloyd Garrison, also fought for the freedom and equality of women.

to make small but regular donations to her Missions' Fund. But Lucy Stone sent her pennies to Boston for a subscription to Garrison's new antislavery newspaper, *The Liberator.* This she smuggled into the students' reading room. Suspected, although not caught in the act, Lucy was summoned to an interview with Mary Lyon, who warned her: "You must remember that the slavery question is a very grave question, and one upon which the best people are divided." This unpleasantness, plus the death of her sister and her mother's ill health, brought an end to Lucy Stone's stay at Mount Holyoke.

While at home running the household, the London incident gave an intense purpose to the life of Lucy Stone. The eviction of Lucretia Mott and Elizabeth Stanton from the London convention received world-wide publicity and unleashed a force which made at first hundreds, then thousands of women acutely aware of their status. At the time, they had no rallying point, but Lucy Stone would eventually provide it.

In 1838, Ohio's Oberlin College became the first coeducational institution of higher learning in America, and in the fall of 1843, Lucy Stone matriculated. Oberlin was also the first college in the Middle West to admit Negroes. Lucy Stone wrote in a letter to her mother, "Colored gentlemen and ladies sit at the same table with us, and there appears to be no difference."

In spite of Oberlin's reputation as a liberal college, Lucy Stone did not have the complete approval of the faculty and their wives. During her second year at the school, she formed the first girls' debating society in America. She said at the organization meeting, "We shall leave this college with a reputation of a thoroughly collegiate course, yet not one of us could state a question or argue it in successful debate. For this reason I have proposed the formation of this association."

Lucy Stone learned to "state a question and debate it" so successfully that the Negro students invited her to speak at their celebration in honor of West Indian independence. (The other speaker was Oberlin's President Mahan). This shocking example of female immodesty brought a reprimand from a committee of faculty wives, which had about as much effect upon Lucy Stone as water on a duck's back.

By 1848, Lucy Stone's platform presence, backed by complete self-confidence, led her to choose public speaking and lecturing as a career. The "public lecturer" was popular from the 1840's to the turn of the twentieth century. He thrived on the need of the middle class to "improve its mind." People wanted to know a little more than what they had learned in eight grades or less of school. They wanted to hear public issues discussed (provided the speaker agreed with their ideas). They wanted to learn about new scientific inventions, and about new theories in medicine and religion. Their lecturer was the forerunner of the Chautauqua and later, educational TV. And so such men as Horace Greeley, editor of the New York *Tribune*; Henry Ward Beecher, the spectacular preacher of Brooklyn's Plymouth Church; Morse of the telegraph, Maury, the greatest oceanographer of the time; and Professor Lowe of balloon fame, criss-crossed the country lecturing.

In reply to a letter from her mother opposing Lucy's career as a "public lecturer," she wrote, "there are no trials so great as they suffer who neglect or refuse to do what they believe is their duty. I expect to plead not for the slave only, but for suffering humanity everywhere. *Especially do I mean to labor for the elevation of my sex.*"

Immediately upon receiving her degree from Oberlin,

Lucy Stone was asked to lecture for the Anti-Slavery Societies of Massachusetts and Ohio, the latter representing most of the Midwest. In the summer of 1848, Lucy faced her first mob. In a talk at Harwich, Massachusetts, she was roughed up by a crowd of hoodlums whose yells, she said, could be heard for a mile. The speaker's platform was wrecked and her clothing torn. But after this "baptism of fire" she never flinched.

She was not an orator in the popular sense. Her delivery was too simple, logical, and sincere. But crowds listened even when they disagreed with her. And she was a master at handling hecklers. On one occasion when she was speaking on woman's rights, a man yelled, "Hey, Lucy, how would you like to be a man?" Miss Stone replied quietly, "I wouldn't. How would you?"

Just as the Grimké sisters had irritated Garrison's Abolitionists in 1838 by mixing woman's rights with slavery, the Massachusetts Anti-Slavery Society felt strongly that Lucy Stone's lectures, which were attracting greater crowds monthly, were subversive in that they linked the problems of the South Carolina Negro with those of the New England female textile worker.

Lucy Stone had been greatly inspired by sculptor Hiram Powers's statue, *Greek Slave,* which today rests in Washington's Corcoran Art Gallery. Lucy saw it exhibited in Boston. *Greek Slave,* although representing a nude girl, was so sensitively done that even women of the Victorian Era, who put ruffled skirts on piano legs, were seldom shocked by it. The slave is a Greek girl of about eighteen. She is half-sitting, half-crouching. There are chains on her wrists. She does not show fear — only quiet, hopeless subjection.

After seeing the statue, Lucy commented, *"Greek Slave* took hold of me like Samson before the Gates of Gaza. I said, 'Mr. May (an Abolitionist minister who had criticized her lectures), I was a woman before I was an Abolitionist. I must speak for women. I will not lecture any more for the Anti-Slavery Society, but will work wholly for woman's rights.' "

A compromise was reached whereby Lucy Stone would lecture for the Abolitionists on Saturday and Sunday nights. This was a practical solution, since Puritan New England held that the Sabbath began at sundown on Saturday and ended Monday at sunrise. Obviously no church or public building would be available for anything as secular as woman's rights on those nights.

During the following years, Lucy Stone was a complete "loner" in her struggle. There was no national or even regional woman suffrage organization. Lucretia Mott and Elizabeth Stanton were still nursing their London wounds, but were not instigating action of any kind.

Lucy said of her lonely campaign, "When I undertook my solitary battle for woman's rights, outside a little circle of Abolitionists, I knew nobody who sympathized with my ideas. I had some handbills printed, 12 by 10 inches. I bought a paper of tacks, and, as I could not pay for posting, I put up my bills myself, using a rock for a hammer. I did not take a fee at the door. But there was always the expense of the hall and hotel. To cover this, at the close of my speech, I asked for help for the great work by a collection for expenses. Then I took a hat and went through the audience for the collection, for all were strangers to me. I always got enough to pay what was due, and sometimes more."

While Lucy Stone was able to quell the male hecklers at her meetings, she was unable to prevent a hostile press from vilifying her character at every opportunity. After a lecture in Indiana, a morning paper reported that she had been seen in a saloon, smoking a cigar and swearing like a trooper. The Springfield (Massachusetts) *Republican* wrote, "You she-hyena, don't you come here."

Most people were surprised when they first heard and saw Lucy Stone. As a champion of woman's rights, they expected to see a tall, gaunt, masculine-appearing woman with a loud, harsh voice. But Lucy Stone was a small, gentle woman, carefully poised, with a voice that became famous. Her daughter and biographer, Alice Stone Blackwell, described that voice: "It was so musical and delicious that those who had once listened to her, if they heard her speak a few words years afterward, on a railroad train or in a stagecoach where it was too dark to see faces, would say unhesitatingly, 'That is Lucy Stone.'"

On May 1, 1885, Lucy Stone, after long consideration, took time out from a lecture tour to marry Henry Blackwell, one of the few prominent males who had defended woman's rights. Henry Blackwell became a prosperous businessman and devoted most of his wealth to Lucy's cause. The keynote to this happy union was a most unusual part of the marriage ceremony. Instead of the traditional "Love, honor, and obey," the couple read in unison aloud, "Protest." This "Protest," really a marriage contract, contained the following:

"While we acknowledge our mutual affection by publicly assuming the relationship of husband and wife, yet, in justice to ourselves and a great principle, we deem it a duty to declare that this act on our part implies no sanction of, nor promise of voluntary obedience to such of the present laws of marriage as refuse to recognize the wife as an independent, rational being, while they confer upon the husband an unnatural superiority, investing him with legal powers which no honorable man should possess. We protest especially against laws which give to the husband:

1. The custody of the wife's person.
2. The exclusive control and guardianship of their children.
3. The sole ownership of her personal property and use of her real estate, unless previously settled upon her, or placed in the hands of trustees, as in the case of lunatics, minors and idiots.
4. The absolute right to the product of her industry.
5. Also against laws which give power to the widower so much larger and more permanent interest in the property of the deceased wife than they give to the widow.
6. Finally, against the whole system by which the legal existence of the wife is suspended during marriage, so that, in most states, she neither has a legal part in the choice of her residence, nor can she make a will, nor sue or be sued in her own name, nor inherit property.

"We believe that personal independence and equal human rights can never be forfeited, except for crime; that marriage should be an equal and permanent partnership, and so recognized by law; that until it is so recognized, married partners should provide against the radical injustice of the present laws by every means in their power.

"Thus reverencing law, we enter our earnest protest against rules and customs which are unworthy of the name, since they violate justice, the essence of all law."

This bizarre opening of an 1855 wedding ceremony was widely publicized, and brought forth the expected newspaper comments. The Washington *Union* said: "We understand that Mr. Blackwell, who last fall assaulted a Southern lady and stole her slave [he actually only assisted her fugitive slave, with no violence], has married Lucy Stone. Justice, though sometimes tardy, never fails to overtake the victim."

Nevertheless, this marriage contract between Henry Blackwell and Lucy Stone (she refused to be known legally as Lucy Blackwell) represented the philosophies of both partners on the rights of women. Its terms were to become the platform of woman suffrage organizations for the next seventy years. Paragraph by paragraph, the Stone-Blackwell marriage contract was gradually to become the law of the land. Greater names were to dominate the woman's rights conventions in the years following the Civil War, but they would all be following the lead of quiet, pretty Lucy Stone, who started the Great Crusade — all by herself.

3   *On to Worcester*

There had been a woman's rights convention at Seneca Falls, New York, in 1848. Some historians mark this gathering as the birth of the organized movement for woman's rights. Others do not concede that it accomplished anything permanent. However, the Woman's Rights Convention of 1848 accomplished two things which were to be landmarks in the struggle. First, the delegates passed a resolution that thoroughly shocked male America: "It is the duty of the women of this country to secure their sacred right to the elective franchise."

This was the first time that a meeting of prominent women had agreed on suffrage as one of their prime goals. Little had been said about it at previous gatherings of women, and it is not likely that everyone at the Seneca Falls convention voted for the resolution. But at Seneca Falls, "Votes for Women!" was heard, and it would be heard until August 26, 1920.

The second important feature of the Seneca Falls convention was that it brought together three women who were to be the trinity of the movement: Lucretia Mott, Elizabeth

Cady Stanton, and Susan B. Anthony. Susan Anthony was a new recruit to the woman suffrage cause, but she had been a fighter for woman's legal and social rights ever since her first schoolteaching experience when she found that a male teacher was receiving forty dollars a month and doing the same work for which she was paid ten. At a time when women, like children, were to be seen and not heard, she addressed a meeting of the New York State Teachers' Association and demanded equal pay for men and women. At the age of twenty-seven, she became involved in the temperance movement, which led to her first lesson on the political status of women.

Susan came to Albany, New York, with a petition bearing 28,000 signatures, asking the legislature to tighten the laws governing the liquor industry. Presenting the petition to an

Susan B. Anthony, a young school teacher, was recruited to the suffrage cause when she found herself earning one-fourth the salary of a male teacher.

assemblyman, she got the retort: "Who are all these signers? Nothing but women!" Susan Anthony's answer was short: "A woman's name on a petition will never be as good as a man's until she has the vote."

But Seneca Falls lacked a follow-through. It founded no permanent organization. Men were shocked by the suffrage resolution, which received wide publicity. But with no organization to back it up, it was merely an opinion of the convention, a convention which only filled Elizabeth Stanton's living room. It would be two years before the woman's rights movement, if it could be so called at the time, would begin to develop a focused purpose. In the meantime, the ladies scattered their shots at liquor, slavery, women's working conditions, and all varieties of feminist causes.

Then in the spring of 1850, a great antislavery convention was held in Boston. Garrison, Wendell Phillips, and Lucy Stone were on the speakers' platform. Due to Lucy's prodding, an unusually large number of women delegates were present. Under her leadership, a meeting of women delegates was held at the end of the convention, and there she launched her plan for a National Woman's Rights Convention to be held during the year. A committee of seven was chosen to select a time and place for the convention, and to issue a call.

As Lucy Stone later said: "We talked the matter over and decided that it was time something was done for the women as well as the Negroes, and the best way to do it was to hold a convention. We did not know how much cooperation we would have. The antislavery people were all full of their own work, but Mr. Garrison, Wendell Phillips, Gerrit Smith, Henry Wright and most of the Abolitionists, who were on the side of Mr. Garrison, were in favor of equal rights for women. We had not any money or any organization, and the question arose, 'How are we ever to make this convention known?' We agreed that we would divide the correspondence. Some would write to one state, and some to another, to see whom we could unite in calling the convention."

Then Miss Stone called on Garrison for advice. He was encouraging. He reminded her that the Abolitionist movement had been launched without funds, and he offered her the use of his vast mailing list. Soon the "Call to convention" was in the mails. Lucy Stone headed the list of signers, followed by eighty-nine distinguished men and women from six states. Among them was Ralph Waldo Emerson. The convention was called for October 25, in Brinley Hall, Worcester, Massachusetts.

October 25, 1850, was a great day in the life of Lucy Stone. Again she had done it alone. In comparison with the Seneca Falls convention, held in the home of Elizabeth Stanton, the New York *Tribune* reported: "Above a thousand persons were present, and, if a larger place could have been had, many more thousands would have attended." On the platform as speakers were Lucy Stone, Lucretia Mott, Garrison, Dr. Martha Mowry, Phillips, several other "greats" of the day who have been forgotten, and a new-comer to the cause of woman's rights, the eminent Negro orator, Frederick Douglass.

Frederick Douglass was born a slave on a plantation near Easton, Maryland. He could never be sure, but he thought he was born around 1818. In 1838, he escaped and reached New Bedford, Massachusetts. In order to avoid detection under the Fugitive Slave Law, he dropped his former master's name and assumed that of Frederick Douglass, because the Douglas clan of Scotland was noted for its bravery. Educating himself, he joined William Garrison in

Frederick Douglass, escaped slave and famous orator, was an abolitionist who also crusaded for the rights of women.

lecturing against slavery. With a fine voice, good diction and eloquence, he could dramatize the slave-owner's lash with the real scars on his own back. By 1843, he was a popular lecturer throughout the North, and in 1845, his autobiography became a best-seller. The following year, he lectured throughout England.

At Lucy Stone's National Woman's Rights Convention, Frederick Douglass was partially repaying the debt of the Abolitionist to the efforts women had devoted to the freedom of the slave. In 1872, he was to overpay the balance by permitting himself to become involved in the most bizarre performance in the American history of woman's rights.

When the first National Woman's Rights Convention was over, the women had listened to hours of oratory and had done little that would have an immediate effect. However, the meeting had some positive results. It had received world-wide publicity, much of it favorable, thanks to Horace Greeley's New York *Tribune*. The London newspapers gave the convention a warm reception, and soon Lucy Stone was receiving letters of congratulation from British woman's rights leaders, testifying how much the Worcester meeting had done to encourage their movement. Particularly encouraging to Lucy Stone was the vote just before adjournment to make the National Woman's Rights Convention an annual event, and so it was until the Civil War.

The Worcester Convention had a number of concrete results, the first in the history of the movement. It inspired organization at the state level, particularly in New York and Ohio. It brought support from some of the best male brains in the nation, and it moved some legislators to take the women seriously.

That same year the Woman's Rights Society of Ohio met at Salem. One speaker reviewed the grievances of women throughout the world. She referred to the plight of Siberian women who were not allowed to step across the footsteps of a man or a reindeer; and the Turkish women who, along with dogs and pigs, were not allowed to enter a mosque.

Woman's rights conventions were beginning to attract an ever-growing number of men, but the men who attended the Salem convention might just as well have stayed at home. This convention was completely officered by women, and not a man was on the platform. Elizabeth Stanton, who was present, reported, *"Never did men so suffer. They im-*plored just to say a word; but no, the president was inflexible — no man should be heard. If one meekly rose to make a suggestion, he was immediately ruled out of order. For the first time in history, men learned how it felt to sit in silence when questions in which they were interested were under discussion. However, the gentlemen in the convention passed through this severe trial with calm resignation; and at the close, organized an association of their own and generously endorsed all the ladies had said and done."

A plucky woman, who was inspired to fight for woman suffrage in her home state of Vermont, was Clarinda Howard Nichols. She had already gained national fame from her successful campaign for property rights. In 1843, with no previous experience, she took over the editorship of the Windham County *Democrat*, because of her husband's crippling illness. In 1847, she started a series of editorials "setting forth the injustice and miserable economy of the property disabilities of women." Clarinda Nichols's editorials were so forceful and persuasive that they moved State Senator Larkin Meade of Brattleboro to introduce a woman's property rights bill in the Vermont Senate. Meade's bill,

Clarina I. Howard Nichols edited her sick husband's newspaper. She promoted property rights for women.

the first of its kind in the country, passed both houses of the legislature, and was signed into law by the governor. Mrs. Nichols said, "This was the first breath of a legal existence for Vermont wives."

Next, Clarinda Nichols started her campaign for woman suffrage. Knowing the opposition she faced, she began modestly by getting two hundred prominent Vermont business men to sign a petition asking the legislature to authorize women to vote in school district meetings. Mrs. Nichols explained her strategy: "In this cautious way I proceeded, aware that not a house would be opened to me if I demand suffrage before convicting men of legal robbery through woman's inability to protect herself." Clarinda knew her Vermonters.

Mrs. Nichols also knew that she would be lampooned by her chief rival, the Rutland *Herald,* and she knew that ridicule is a very powerful weapon. For counsel she sought out the Speaker of the Vermont House of Representatives. It was his suggestion that she come to Montpelier. He would suggest to the House that she be invited to speak for her petition, and he predicted that she would be invited to speak "by a handsome vote." The "handsome vote" was just that. There was only one "Nay," cast by the chairman of the Education Committee, who said, "If the lady wants to make herself ridiculous, let her come and make herself as ridiculous as possible, as soon as possible, but I don't believe in the scramble for pants."

Mrs. Nichols was in the House gallery while the "invitation vote" was taken. Then she immediately came down to the Speaker's rostrum. But before beginning to read her prepared speech on the platform, which was later rejected by the House, she said in a firm, even voice, "Since my husband owns my skirts, why should I not seek pants?"

The 1851 National Woman's Rights Convention, again organized by Lucy Stone, returned to Worcester. It was remarkable only for the volume of oratory. The third convention was held in Syracuse, New York, September 8, 9, and 10, 1852. The Syracuse *Daily Star* welcomed the delegates thus: "The Women Are Coming! They flock in on us from every quarter, all to hear and talk about woman's rights. The blue-stockings are as thick as grasshoppers in hay-time, and mighty will be the 'jaw-logic' and 'broomstick ethics' preached by the *females of both sexes.*"

At the Syracuse convention, Susan B. Anthony was the principal speaker, and from that year on, she was to be the guiding force of woman's rights conventions. Lucy Stone was again going it alone, and Lucretia Mott becoming the aging symbol of the cause.

There was one sensation at the Syracuse convention which attracted more attention from the press than Susan Anthony's speech. It was the "Bloomer dress," and several women wore it, including Lucy Stone. The Bloomer dress was designed by Mrs. Elizabeth Miller, daughter of the arch-Abolitionist, Gerrit Smith. Mrs. Amelia Bloomer, editor of a woman's magazine, *Lily*, started a crusade for the new costume, and her name became associated with it. The Bloomer dress had no skirt. Instead, the lady's "limbs," as legs were called in Victorian 1852, were encased in loose-fitting pantaloons of ankle length. The Bloomer, in this day of above-the-knee skirts, sounds pretty silly. But it didn't to the woman of 1852, with her long heavy skirts brushing the streets (in the age of the horse), her waist pinched by whalebone corsets, and a high neck even in summer. The Bloomer girl was asserting her right to be almost comfortable. As might be expected, the Bloomer dress inspired almost as many jokes as Prohibition in the 1920's.

The Bloomer Costume.

The best gags are usually factual, and this one involving the Bloomer dress came from Dr. Mary Walker, a Washington physician of the period who adopted the garb. Dr. Walker, considered eccentric, as was any woman who entered the medical profession in the 1850's, nevertheless traveled in the upper levels of Washington society, and according to our correspondent E. Ben Perley:Moore, was frequently present at White House receptions during the administration of President Pierce. She later was commissioned an assistant surgeon in the Union Army. Dr. Walker recounted that once she went on a rather long trip by horse and buggy. Becoming temporarily lost, while touring in her bloomers, she asked a farmer, "Is this the way to Wareham?" Reply: "Dunno, ma'm. I never seen 'em on a woman afore."

During the Syracuse convention, a letter was received from Horace Greeley which was read to the delegates. Greeley counseled that before too much energy was expended on suffrage, more time should be devoted to higher-skilled employment for women. He advocated better schools of dress design. He said that the delegates who complained about wages for female labor should consider "what they are paying maids and cleaning women in their own homes."

With the adjournment of the Syracuse convention, the clergy cut loose. They charged that woman's rights leaders were trying to supersede the influence of the church. They referred to the leaders as infidels. A minister from nearby Auburn bragged: "No member of my congregation is tainted by the unholy doctrine of woman's rights." The Rev. Byron Sutherland of the Plymouth Congregational Church of Syracuse preached a sermon on "The Bloomer Convention," and took his text from Deuteronomy: "The woman shall not wear that which pertaineth to man; neither shall a man put on a woman's garment; for all that do so are an abomination to the Lord thy God."

When Dr. Harriet K. Hunt returned from Syracuse to her home in Boston, she found her tax bill waiting. Fired-up by the oratory of the convention, she stomped into the office of the Boston Tax Collector. First, she slapped down a check for the amount of the bill. Then she drew from her doctor's bag a statement which she read to an astounded tax collector, who listened meekly. It read in part:

"Harriet K. Hunt, physician, a native and permanent resident of the City of Boston, and for many years a tax-payer therein, in making payment of taxes for the coming year, begs leave to protest against the injustice and inequality of levying taxes upon women, and at the same time refusing them any voice or vote in the imposition and expenditure of the same. . . . Even drunkards, felons, idiots and lunatics, if men, may still enjoy that right of voting to which no woman, however large the amount of taxes she pays, however respectable her character, or useful her life, can ever attain."

Dr. Hunt's protest was well publicized, and eventually made a dent in Massachusetts' consistent discrimination against women. Since 1848, there had been repeated petitions to the legislature to forsake the old English common law attitude on woman's property rights. In 1854, when the Whig Party was on its deathbed, and the Massachusetts' Democrats were divided over slavery, the Know-Nothing Party, an organization which was anti-Catholic, anti-Semitic, anti-immigration and anti-everything else, came into power and passed a law securing the property rights of all women married after its passage.

And so the National Woman's Rights Conventions went

on through the fall of 1860. The minutes of those conclaves are dull reading, and the reader wonders how the delegates kept awake. Elizabeth Stanton and Susan Anthony were still the guiding lights. But more important during this period, these two leaders were appearing regularly at hearings of state legislative committees. They were beginning to develop political know-how and the ability to parry ridicule, especially when it came from their own sex.

On one occasion, Elizabeth Stanton was addressing the New York State Assembly, sitting as a committee-of-the-whole. After her speech, she was approached by a group of society matrons who had been sitting in the gallery. In superciliously congratulating Mrs. Stanton, one woman said, "But what do you do with your children?" "Ladies," Elizabeth said, "it takes me no longer to speak than you to listen. What have you been doing with your children the two hours you have been sitting here?"

At another time, Miss Anthony was presiding at a woman's rights convention in Newport, Rhode Island. Newport was rapidly becoming a society resort. After one of the convention sessions, some wealthy ladies who were not participants told Miss Anthony that their objections to the woman's rights movement were the conventions with their blatant publicity, and the immodesty of a woman speaking from a platform.

Susan Anthony has recorded her quick-on-the-trigger reply. "Really," said I, "you surprise me. Our conventions are not as public as the ballroom where I saw you dancing last night. As to modesty, it may be a question in many minds whether it is less modest to speak words of soberness and truth, plainly dressed, on a platform, than gorgeously arrayed with bare arms and shoulders, to waltz in the arms of a strange gentleman."

However, Miss Anthony met her match in 1856 when she appeared before the Judiciary Committee of the New York State Assembly to present the annual petition to end legal discrimination against women. The committee accepted the petition and took only a few minutes to report it out with the usual recommendation: "Inexpedient to legislate." In his report, committee chairman Foote said, "The Committee is composed of married and single gentlemen. The bachelors on the Committee, with becoming diffidence, have left the subject pretty much to the married gentlemen. The latter have considered it [the petition] with the aid of the light they have before them, and the experience married life has given them. Thus aided, they are enabled to state that the ladies always have the best place and the choicest tidbits at the table. They have the best seat in the cars [railroad], carriages and sleighs; the warmest place in winter, and the coolest place in summer. A lady's dress costs three times as much as that of a gentleman, and, at the present time, with prevailing fashion, one lady occupies three times as much space in the world as a gentleman.

"It has thus appeared to the married gentlemen of your Committee, that if there is any inequality or oppression in the case, the gentlemen are the sufferers.

"On the whole, the Committee have concluded that they have observed several instances in which the husband and the wife have both signed the petition. In such case, they would recommend the parties to apply for a law authorizing them to exchange clothes, so that the husband may wear the petticoats, and the wife the breeches, and thus indicate to their neighbors and the public the true relation to which they stand to each other."

The tenth annual Woman's Rights National Convention adjourned in the fall of 1860 after endorsing Abraham

Lincoln for the Presidency, its delegates not knowing that the convention would never meet again; that within eleven months there would be a mobilized Confederate States of America; that few would give any thought to woman's rights during the next five years; and that a new American woman would emerge. after Appomattox.

Since Seneca Falls in 1848, twelve years, the woman's rights leaders had been in high gear. There had been volumes of speeches delivered, hundreds of state and local conventions and petitions to legislatures. In the area of property rights, some progress had been made — toward suffrage, none.

4 *The Bloody Interlude*

The guns which shelled Fort Sumter struck fear of other than the Confederacy in the hearts of Lucy Stone, Susan Anthony, and the other woman's rights leaders. After ten years of national conventions, would there be any more? Wouldn't the energies of the women leaders be directed toward the War and the end of slavery, rather than toward woman's rights?

Their fears were justified. There were no national conventions between 1860 and 1866. Julia Ward Howe, the New England suffrage leader, was spending much time in Washington, where she wrote "The Battle Hymn of the Republic." Hariet Beecher Stowe, another suffragist, was giving much from her royalties on *Uncle Tom's Cabin* to war relief, and most of the other crusaders for Woman's rights were busy with war work of one kind or another.

But a new trend rapidly developed which was to do more for the women than ten years of tub-thumping speeches at the conventions. And it would do it again in 1917. When President Lincoln issued his first call for 75,000 volunteer troops and federalized the state militia regiments, men

Suffragist Julia Ward Howe wrote the immortal "Battle Hymn of the Republic."

began leaving the factories, the farms, the offices and the printing presses. At first, the factory owners were appalled. The government needed everything and in stupendous quantities. It was inconceivable that women could do what men had done, but they were the only answer — a reluctant answer. At first, only a few were hired, but after the first Battle of Bull Run, it was obvious that the war would be long, and already Lincoln was calling for thousands of additional recruits and vast stores of munitions.

The government first set the example, even though it was an example of necessity. The Treasury Department and the Patent Office stepped up its employment of women clerks. At the latter was a woman who wouldn't be there long, Clara Barton. Then Mrs. Bloomer of the magazine *Lily* told her typesetters to get into uniform and hired women in their places. Soon newspapers everywhere were advertising for women typesetters, even offering to train the unskilled.

In the public schools, women were rapidly replacing men as teachers and drawing salaries almost equal to men. Young boys who had been taught by men, were at first embarrassed at being under the tutelage of a "school marm." A story which was widely circulated by the press at the time, involved a "school marm" in Vermont:

Teacher: Johnny, what does b-e-n-c-h spell?

Johnny: Dunno.

Teacher: You are just plain stupid, Johnny. What are you sitting on?

Johnny: If you don't mind, Marm, I'd rather not say, right here in class.

Women doctors, some angels, some quacks, began practicing in ever-increasing numbers, treating only women and children, of course. In a day when professional ethics did not prevent doctors from advertising, if they wanted to, the following ad ran for the year 1864 in the Manchester (New Hampshire) *Dollar Weekly & Mirror* (it cost a dollar a year):

RETURNED

Miss Dr. S. A. Colby

Eclectic Physician

267 Elm St.

Miss Colby having returned from her "Western Tour," has recently taken a beautiful office at the above mentioned place, where she will be happy to meet all her old friends and many new ones; and trusts by devoting all her energies to the "Profession," that she will receive in the future that unqualified success which has crowned her efforts in the past. Diseases of the Head, Lungs, Heart, Liver, Stomach, Kidneys, Spine and Blood, treated with much skill.

Office hours from 2 to 6 and 7 to 9

As the Union regiments were marching through Washington, from the Baltimore & Ohio railroad station and over Long Bridge into Virginia, a clerk in the U.S. Patent Office was experiencing frustration. With limited billeting facilities, the army was housing men in the Patent Office at night. This woman clerk noticed how many of these young men, unaccustomed to marching with wet feet and eating tainted beef, were falling ill. The army medical orderlies, who were treating these men, were coarse, impatient, and rough. She felt that a woman's understanding of these boys, away from home for the first time, could make them get well faster, provided the woman was properly trained in hospital techniques. The Patent Office clerk was Clara Barton.

Clara Barton was born in Oxford, Massachusetts, in 1830. She became a clerk in the Patent Office in 1854, which would indicate that she was a political appointee, and therefore a Buchanan Democrat. Convinced that she had a "call," she obtained an interview with President Lincoln and suggested to him that she organize a corps of women to staff the army field hospitals under the command of army surgeons. Lincoln thanked her, but shook his head. He felt that an army field hospital was no place for a woman. Soldiers were coarse in their language, he reminded Clara. They might get the "wrong idea" of women hovering around their cots. Worse than that, practically every wound in the arm or leg meant amputation, often without anesthesia. Could a woman stand those agonizing screams? Could

During the Civil War, Clara Barton organized a nurse's corps. She founded the American Red Cross Society in 1881.

she stomach the stench of gangrene? No, Mr. Lincoln didn't think so.

Then a determined Clara Barton told Lincoln of Florence Nightingale. Clara's idol probably got her surname from her birth in Florence, Italy, in May, 1820. Florence Nightingale was the daughter of a wealthy Englishman. As a teen-ager, she studied mathematics and science with her father at a time when young ladies weren't supposed to know about such things. Interested in hospital care, Florence, with her father's consent and checkbook, toured Europe, visiting hospitals, observing hospital routine. In 1851, she completed a nurse's training course at Kaiserwerth, Germany.

Then came the Crimean War and the "Charge of the Light Brigade." Florence Nightingale arrived at Scutari in the Crimea on November 4, 1854, with thirty British trained nurses. Her reception by the British "brass" was what might be expected, since the British male's opinion of female competence was no higher than that of his American male cousin. But by 1856, Florence Nightingale was in charge of all British army hospitals in the Crimea, and had received the Victoria Cross from her Queen.

Abraham Lincoln capitulated, and Clara Barton went into the field hospitals of the Army of the Potomac. By 1864, she was in charge of all hospitals and nurses on the James River where Grant was slugging out the last phase of the war. That same year, Congress recognized Clara Barton by voting her $15,000 for relief work on the field, for organizing searches for the wounded, and for marking graves. Clara Barton was now a national figure, and her prestige was to bolster the woman suffrage crusade in the years after the war; but, just as important to the cause, she made the RN a respected professional person and opened a new area of employment for qualified women.

Although the national conventions were suspended, while Lucretia Mott and Susan Anthony were totally engaged in war work, and Julia Howe was setting "Mine eyes have seen the glory" to the old song, "We'll hang Jeff Davis to a sour apple tree," a young lady in Philadelphia was preparing to take an unprecedented part in politics and become the youngest feminist leader in the nation.

Anna Elizabeth Dickinson was born October 28, 1842, in Philadelphia, when Lucretia Mott was old enough to have been her grandmother and Lucy Stone could have been her mother. When Anna Dickinson was only nineteen, and employed at the U.S. Mint in Philadelphia, she began making public appearances, speaking for temperance and against slavery. Because of her political independence, she lost her job at the Mint. There was no Civil Service, and her federal employment was at the mercy of her state's party chairman. A natural public speaker, Anna Dickinson

Anna Emily Dickinson was only nineteen when she first took the stump for women's rights.

turned to the lecture platform, still attacking slavery, the liquor traffic, and ignoring woman's rights.

At this late date, it is impossible to read Anna Dickinson's thoughts in 1862, but they seem to have run something like this: Susan Anthony and Lucy Stone have been campaigning up and down the country, speaking for woman's political rights, but they never get their feet wet in practical politics at the male level. Why don't I try it and show the men that a woman can be politically effective?

And so in the 1863 state election campaigns in New York State and New England, we find Anna Dickinson publicly campaigning for Republican candidates. That the Republican males welcomed her with open arms is attested to by a news dispatch in the Hartford *Courant,* which was copied by newspapers throughout New England: that at the end the the campaign, Anna Dickinson was paid $500 by the Connecticut Republican State Committee for her speaking engagements. And Anna Dickinson could neither vote nor hold office.

In addition to her political speeches, Anna was much in demand for speaking at patriotic rallies. On the night of December 31, 1863, she had the opportunity she had been secretly waiting for. It was a great set-up for her to launch herself as the youngest leader of the woman's rights movement. There was a great "watch night" celebration at Boston's Tremont Temple, because, at the stroke of midnight, Lincoln's Emancipation Proclamation would become effective. There was a long list of speakers, including Frederick Douglass and William Lloyd Garrison. Julia Howe was there to hear the vast crowd sing her "Battle Hymn" as the stroke of twelve sounded, and at the end of the list of speakers was Anna Dickinson.

Speech after speech hailed the Negro's freedom. The goal of the Abolitionists had been won after a battle of over thirty long years. But the job wouldn't be finished, they said, until the Negro had the vote. Finally, Anna Dickinson's turn came. At the outset, she followed the lead of the others, extolling freedom for the blacks and urging their enfranchisement. But then she struck the blow she had been waiting for: the battle for freedom in the United States would not finally be won until "women are free and have the vote." The crowd rose to its feet, and Anna Dickinson had proved herself not only a great spellbinder, but a masterful feminine political strategist.

Now comes one of the most fantastic and apparently hitherto untold stories of the war. After twenty years of Civil War research, this author stumbled upon it purely by accident, but the tale is fully documented and is in the archives of Congress. For practical reasons it was a well-kept secret for years after Lincoln's assassination, even the Presidents who immediately succeeded him did not know of it.

Anna Ella Carroll lived in Maryland. She was a descendant of Charles Carroll of Carrollton, signer of the Declaration of Independence. Her wealthy father had been Governor of Maryland. Socially prominent, she traveled extensively, and in September, 1861, two months after the disaster at Bull Run, she visited St. Louis. There she met a group of young navy officers who were attached to a fleet of gunboats, waiting to begin an attempt to open the Mississippi River to military transportation from St. Louis to New Orleans. Anna Carroll dined and danced with the young officers, never revealing that her greatest interest

Anna Ella Carroll made a hobby of military strategy, and her secret plan was said to have altered the entire Mississippi campaign during the Civil War.

was the study of military strategy, a most unheard of pursuit for a debutante in 1861.

One day, the officers escorted Anna down to the river front where the gunboats were docked. After showing her through a couple of the gunboats, they took her to a chart-room and showed her the plans for the Mississippi campaign, which gives a good idea of security precautions in 1861. They were somewhat surprised when Anna Carroll sat down with the maps and studied them minutely. But they rocked back on their heels when Anna looked up and said, *"Gentlemen, this won't work."*

Needless to say, Anna Carroll had no more dates with the navy, but now she had something else in mind. She packed her horsehair trunk and hurried back to Maryland. There she buried herself in maps and topographical charts of Kentucky, Tennessee, and Georgia. She studied with a map in one hand, and in the other, her copy of Dufour's *Strategy and Tactics,* the West Point textbook of the time, Now she was tracing her maps and marking routes of marches, supply depots, railroad junctions, and artillery placements.

Thomas A Scott, Lincoln's Assistant Secretary of War, was a friend of Anna Carroll, and soon he received a call from her. When she entered his office, she came to the point immediately and spread out her charts. Scott was not quite as shocked as the young ensigns in St. Louis, since he had known of Anna's hobby, but he seriously doubted that her military judgment was superior to that of Ulysses S. Grant and William Tecumseh Sherman who had planned the Mississippi campaign and who had the approval of the President. But he politely told Anna that he would examine her plan. Then the more he studied Anna's strategy, the better it looked. It seemed so logical, that he took her charts to Secretary of War, Edwin M. Stanton. The latter, who liked neither Grant nor Sherman, said he was greatly impressed, and told Scott that he would accompany him to the White House.

In the Cabinet room, Abraham Lincoln put on his steel-rimmed spectacles and spread out Anna Carroll's charts and notes. After a few minutes, the President sent a messenger to summon General Henry W. Halleck, his Chief of Staff. All agreed Anna's plan was practical and more sure of success than that planned by Grant. However, they faced a great dilemma. How could they approve a military campaign planned by a woman? What if the campaign should fail, and it should become known that Lincoln had accepted Anna Carroll's strategy over Grant's? The country would judge him insane or a traitor. There would be a grueling investigation. And that meant that one other man must be in on the secret, Senator Ben Wade of Ohio, president *pro tem* of the Senate and chairman of the Joint Committee on the Conduct of War, the committee which would investigate should the campaign fail. Soon Wade was at the White House and approved the plan, and it was about the only issue on which Wade was to agree with the President during the war. But Ben Wade, a rough-and-tumble politician, possessing a strong vengeance, strangely enough had less prejudice against women than any man in the Senate at the time. In later years, he was to be one of the first supporters of woman suffrage.

Anna Carroll's plan was approved — a plan which, in broad terms, led to Grant's victory at Ft. Donelson, the capture of Vicksburg, and Sherman's march to the sea. But now the quintet — Lincoln, Halleck, Wade, Stanton, and Scott swore themselves to absolute secrecy. No one, the military, the public, or Congress must ever know where

Belle Boyd was a beautiful confederate spy.

the plan originated. The secret was· kept. Lincoln and Stanton died with it. Scott held his tongue, and the secret was not divulged by Wade until he told it years later to support a bill for woman suffrage.

There were other heroines of the Civil War who dramatized female ability — the woman spies. There was the Secret Service operative, Carrie Lawton, who spent weeks in Richmond obtaining the Confederate plans for the campaign against McClellan; Belle Boyd, who gave Stonewall Jackson the information with which he could drive federal troops out of the Shenandoah Valley; Rebecca Wright, the Quaker girl who helped General Sheridan to retake the Valley; and the greatest spy of them all, Confederate Rose O'Neal Greenhow, who drank claret in her

Washington home with Union Army officers and congressional leaders.

Yes, Dickinson, Barton, Howe, Carroll, Lawton, Boyd, and Greenhow were the "glamour girls" of the Civil War. They attracted the attention and admiration of the American male. But the women who would provide impetus in the crusade for woman's rights in the next thirty-five years were those, who from 1861 to 1865 had threaded the factory looms, cured the sick, nursed the wounded, kept the newspapers running, tapped the telegraph keys, stitched the uniforms, taught the schools, and managed the farms.

These women would no longer tolerate beatings by their husbands who bought liquor with their wages. They would not give up property which they had rightfully inherited. They would demand equal custody of their children, and eventually, *they would vote!*

5   *The Postwar Woman*

As soon as Robert E. Lee and Ulysses S. Grant had shaken
hands at Appomattox, the woman's rights leaders, Elizabeth
Stanton and Susan Anthony, now joined by Anna Dickinson,
were back in the fight for suffrage. They knew that the
Negro would be given the vote, and when that legislation
would be under consideration, the women could be included. As soon as the debate on the proposed Fourteenth
Amendment started, petitions began pouring into Washington. They fell on deaf ears, ears deafened by confusion.

The Radical Republicans wanted the Negro to vote
immediately. He would be indebted to the Republican
Party, and could be manipulated by the Yankee "Carpet-
baggers," who poured into the South following the surren-
der, for the economic pillaging of an already prostrate
region and to "make political hay." A few Republican
politicians believed that white women should vote, but
that would include "Southern wenches," as one "freedom-
loving" Northern politician put it. The Northern politician
still believed the white woman to be intellectually inferior
to the white male, and so, to be consistent, he had to place
the Negro woman that much lower on the scale, since he

didn't really believe that the Negro male, for whom he was advocating the vote, was his intellectual equal.

The years 1865-68 were a period of political confusion for Congress, Republicans, Democrats, Abolitionists, Negroes, and the women. Without the male Negroes voting immediately, the Republicans feared the loss of control if President Andrew Johnson rapidly readmitted the Southern states, as Lincoln had planned. To establish a black vote in the South, they couldn't take time to hold lengthy debates on woman suffrage, especially when they didn't know how the women would vote. On the other hand, they were in an embarrassing position. Women leaders, Anna Dickinson for one, had been most effective in campaigning for the Republican ticket. The Women's Loyal Leagues during the war had been solidly Republican-Abolitionist, and they had influenced many votes. Women in the factories and on the farms had helped win the War, and without victory there might have been no Republican Party. The Republicans owed a great political debt to the women. "But what can we do under the circumstances?" they said. "Woman suffrage, at this time, will becloud our chief issue."

From 1848 to Appomattox, the Abolitionist leaders had given support to the women and had received their support in the days when they had few friends, even in the North. But now, at the crucial hour when the Negro franchise was in the balance, after thirty years, how could they divert their energies to becoming embroiled in the women's demands? Woman suffrage, as an issue in Congress, might cause them to lose everything.

The Negroes owed an enormous debt to the woman's rights movement. Since the 1830's, the women had spent more time working for emancipation than they had for woman suffrage. But now the Negro leaders said, "Please don't get in the way until we have won the vote. Then we will support you," and Frederick Douglass, who had been speaking at woman's rights conventions since 1850, was not heard from in the cause until the election campaign of 1872.

Next, the Democrats got into the embroglio. They were without congressional representation in the South, and stood little chance of winning the presidential election in 1868. Some Democratic leaders offered their support to the suffrage movement. Some hesitant "rights" leaders accepted, but immediately these ladies, who had worked incessantly for the defeat of the South and the dominance of the Republican Party, were branded as Copperheads (the copperhead is a poisonous snake found in the South, and its name was applied to antiwar Democrats in the North). Both the Democrats and the women were embarrassed.

And so in the complete political confusion over women in the immediate postwar period, woman's rights were excluded from serious debate on the floors of Congress at a time when the issue might have been settled dramatically and swiftly. Even Senator Sumner, the Harvard intellectual from Massachusetts, who had professed sympathy for the suffrage cause, read under protest in the Senate a petition signed by 300,000 men and women. "Most inopportune," he said.

Fortunately for the collective conscience of Congress, it was very busy. There were war claims to be settled, veterans' pensions, the currency, and laws to subject the South. Nevertheless, some feeble attempts at feminist legislation were put forward. During the second session of the Thirty-ninth Congress, a bill was under debate "to regulate the franchise in the District of Columbia." It was intended to enfranchise the Negro male. On December 10,

1866, Senator Cowan of Pennsylvania rose and moved to amend the bill by striking out the word "male" before the word "person." The debate lasted three days, and the outcome was obvious. Even Horace Greeley's *Tribune*, usually kind to the women, attacked Cowan for introducing the amendment, because the debate would delay the franchise for the Negro in the nation's capital.

Senator Cowan's speech on his amendment was received with hoots by his fellow senators, but it is notable that his principal argument would be heard within a few years in many state legislatures. He said in part: "I do not know anything about manhood which qualifies it more for this purpose [voting] than exists in womanhood. Womanhood to me is rather the more exalted of the two. . . . If you want to widen the franchise so as to purify your ballot box, throw the virtue of the country into it; throw the temperance of the country into it; throw the angel element, if I may so express myself, into it."

After a hiatus of five years, the women went back to their conventions, but now their purpose was somewhat more focused on suffrage — somewhat, but not enough. The names of the leaders of the 1866 convention were familiar: Stanton, Anthony, Dickinson, and aging Lucretia Mott. The principal speaker had just recently joined the cause, but would be one of the most colorful warriors for woman's rights for the next six years, until he became involved in a scandal that rocked Protestant America.

Henry Ward Beecher was without doubt the greatest preacher in America during the nineteenth century. He was the son of another great preacher, Lyman Beecher, and his sister was Harriet Beecher Stowe, author of *Uncle Tom's Cabin*. Having started penniless at a small church in Kentucky, New England-born Henry Ward Beecher had forged

With slavery abolished, Henry Ward Beecher, the most popular preacher of his day, poured his talents into the woman's suffrage cause.

ahead to the great Plymouth Congregational Church of Brooklyn for which he had raised the building fund. His congregation was large and wealthy, but each Sunday, ferries carried hundreds of New York City residents to hear his golden voice. His methods were always spectacular. Prior to the Civil War, while preaching against slavery, he brought to the pulpit escaped beautiful Negro slave girls and auctioned them to buy their freedom. Some of his congregation wondered where he got the girls, but the dollars poured in. One of the most sought-after public speakers, he made a fortune outside the church from his lecture tours.

The 1866 convention followed the pattern of the prewar meetings, but the speeches were longer. No more had been accomplished than in 1860, but now the feminist leaders found a battleground which would test their ability to conduct a practical, effective, political campaign. In 1867, Kansas was to draft and submit to the people a new constitution. Here was a real challenge to roll up an impressive vote for woman suffrage.

Early female arrivals on the Kansas plains in 1867 were encouraged to find a keen interest among many male voters in the franchise for the women of the "Sunflower State." They believed that they could depend upon the Republicans and former Abolitionists for sufficient support to carry a woman suffrage amendment which had been proposed. But though there was individual voter interest, they received no help from the Kansas Republican organization. The Republican governor had endorsed the amendment at the constitutional convention, removing the word "male" from the new draft, but his party refused to urge it upon the voters of the state. The Democrats, who had offered some support to the feminist cause in the East, in Kansas opposed the suffrage amendment, because, they said, the women were also supporting a temperance amendment. Even the Negroes joined the opposition.

The women opened their campaign in July, and all of the national leaders were there. They brought with them the famous Hutchinson Family from New Hampshire, a singing group which had been excluded from the Civil War army camps by General McClellan because they specialized in antislavery songs, and the General did not agree that slavery was the issue of the war. They also brought with them thousands of pamphlets for door-to-door distribution. They began the now familiar technique of organized "letters to the editor." A fund-raising drive soon produced enough money to finance an effective campaign. The spectacular — if eccentric — lawyer, George Francis Train, arrived from New York and pleaded with crowds at rallies "not to lift the Negroes above the heads of your own mothers, wives, sisters and daughters."

On the morning of election day, there was a long suffrage parade in Leavenworth. There was a band, and the Hutchinson family was on a float. Susan Anthony and Elizabeth Stanton rode in barouches. Lucy Stone and her husband, Henry Blackwell, rode in a carriage.

The vote was slow in coming in that night, and all signs pointed to a close result — and close it was. Roughly, the returns were 10,000 for striking "white" from the constitution but retaining "male"; 9,000 for striking out "male." The result was temporarily disheartening, but for the first time since 1790, a woman suffrage measure had been submitted to the voters of an entire state, and the Kansas amendment had come very close to adoption.

But while the suffrage fighters Stanton, Anthony, and Stone were nursing their wounds, a development without leadership was under way which was to be more effective

In Kansas, 1867, lawyer George Francis Train's campaign almost put woman's suffrage into the new state constitution, losing by merely 1,000 votes.

than all the women's conventions since 1848. It was the "postwar woman," and she lived principally in the South and West. There was a "postwar woman" in the East, but she was only doing more of what she had done before.

In the South, former belles who had never thought of anything but a "moonlight-and-honeysuckle" existence were marrying the crippled wrecks who had come home from defeat on the battlefield. Others were managing what was left of the plantations when their husbands didn't come home. Both were rebuilding houses which had been burned by Sherman's army. For the first time, Southern women were staffing the schools, selling goods over the counter, and farming. For the first time, women who managed property were paying taxes, and they were becoming interested in what the county did with their money.

In the East, women were suffering from labor conditions which could only be improved by their votes. In 1865, women were still pouring into industry. The return of the soldiers did not drive the women out of a rapidly expanding industry. But male competition forced women's wages below starvation level. In New York City, there were 15,000 women employed at wages of $2.50 to $3.00 per week, while men were averaging $9.00. The women worked ten hours a day, most as clerks in stores where there were no rest rooms, no place to eat lunch, and they stood all day. Seamstresses who took work home received seventy-five cents to stitch a dozen pairs of overalls.

In this unbearable atmosphere, Susan Anthony temporarily diverted her attention from woman suffrage and became the first president of the Workingwoman's Protective Association. Barred from membership in the rapidly growing, all-male labor organizations, women began forming their own unions in the cigar and shoe industries. Women who learned to bargain with their employers and organize strikes would soon be more effective in fighting for their political rights.

But it was in the "Wild and Wooly West" that the postwar woman reached new heights. One of the most noticeable features in the social climate of the new West was its deference toward women as equals. The freedom of the West and its need for rapid development offered women new job opportunities and responsibilities. Women were so badly needed that they rose to new dignity.

In 1865, there were three men to every woman in California, four to one in Washington, eight to one in Nevada, and *twenty to one in Colorado*. In the Pacific Northwest, the need for a female population was so great that a whole shipload of women was brought by way of Cape Horn to fill the need for teachers, clerks, and housekeepers. According to Allan Nevins in his *The Emergence of Modern America*: "Women were treated not merely as men's equals, but as a strange and costly creation whose whim ought to be law." Women's wages in Denver were four times those of Chicago, and with room and board thrown in. The pioneer Western woman equaled the man in individualism, resourcefulness and courage. With the Western woman in the saddle, literally and figuratively, something had to give — and it did.

The Wyoming Territory was settled by the Mormon leader, Brigham Young, in 1847, when he arrived with 143 men and seventy-five wagons. The following year, 1,200 men, women, and children came. But the federal government took a dim view of the Mormons practicing polygamy, and in 1859, Young and his flock were driven from Wyoming into Utah. The Civil War and hostile Indians temporarily prevented further immigration into the Wyoming

Brigham Young,
Mormon leader, brought
woman suffrage to
Utah in 1870.

Territory, but in 1867, the Union Pacific Railroad reached
what is now Cheyenne, bringing a flood of pioneers. Soon
Wyoming was the wildest of the West. There were more
saloons than homes. Roving gangs shot up towns, there was
brawling in the streets, and the sheriffs were unable to
maintain order without the aid of vigilantes.

Also in 1867, Wyoming elected its first territorial delegate
to Congress, and 1,900 votes were cast. By 1869, 5,266 votes
were cast in the territorial election. But in the preceding
year, the more sober citizens of Wyoming had done some
hard thinking. The present government was not adequate
for the Territory and obviously could not maintain order or
punish crime. The government must be turned out, but

were there enough decent citizens to carry the election? Then they came up with the answer: yes, there were enough *if suffrage was universal.*

In November, 1869, the territorial legislature met to draft a completely new code of laws for Wyoming. It contained a strong definition of woman's rights, legalized gambling, and required a jail for each county. On December 10, a special election was held. Without Susan Anthony, Elizabeth Stanton, or the Hutchinson family, Wyoming voted overwhelmingly for woman suffrage. The voters went even further, making women eligible for jury duty and for appointment as justices of the peace. Immediately after the election, Mrs. Esther Morris, the wife of a prominent businessman, was appointed Justice of the Peace for Cheyenne. Law and order had won, and so had American womanhood. The wall of male prejudice was breached, if only minutely.

The next state to grant woman suffrage was an unlikely one, even though it was in the West. The status of women in Brigham Young's Mormon Church was hardly that of California or Colorado. The Mormon Church was a theocracy, in that it was the government of Utah Territory. All authority lay in the priesthood, and Brigham Young even had his secret police — The Host of Israel. *The Deseret News,* established in 1850, was the official newspaper of Mormonism.

The Mormons referred to other persons, whether Catholics, Protestants, Jews, or Muslims, as Gentiles. Young and his followers at first wanted no Gentiles in Utah. But it was impossible to stop the steady trickle of Western pioneers who would go where they pleased as long as they were quicker on the draw than the other fellow. Thus small pockets of Gentiles were settling in Utah. Then in 1869, the Union Pacific Railroad reached Utah, and the driving of the golden spike at Promontory Point, that same year, linked San Francisco with New York.

At first, Young wanted the railroad to skirt Salt Lake City. He believed in an isolated Mormonism at the time. But the obvious financial gain overcame his isolationism, and soon he was holding out all kinds of inducements to the Union Pacific. With the Union Pacific came a horde of Gentiles. Soon they formed a very forceful minority in Utah and they resented the political control of the Church, so they began organizing political parties. There was one "omnibus party" for all Gentiles. The Liberal Party had but one motive, to combat Mormon control of the territorial government. Then there were Democrats and Republicans to vie for control of the Liberal organization. Of course, all this was upsetting to Brigham Young.

Now the Mormons and the Gentiles seem to have come up with the same idea with the same purpose. The Gentiles apparently thought that if woman suffrage could be permitted, they would nearly double their voting strength, and they didn't believe that Mormon women would be permitted to vote even if they had the right. But the Mormons saw that they could more than double their vote with woman suffrage because some of the male Mormons had as many as six wives. And so in 1870, Utah voted woman suffrage. Two days after the law was passed, there was an election. To the surprise of both factions, only a few women voted, but among them was Seraph Young a niece of Brigham.

On July 28, 1868, Congress passed the Fourteenth Amendment: "All persons born or naturalized in the United

States, and subject to the jurisdiction thereof, are citizens of the United States and of the State wherein they reside. No State shall make or enforce any law which shall abridge the privileges or immunities of citizens of the United States; nor shall any State deprive any person of life, liberty, or property, without due process of law; nor deny to any person within its jurisdiction the equal protection of the laws."

Then on March 30, 1870, Congress passed the Fifteenth Amendment: "The right of citizens of the United States to vote shall not be denied or abridged by the United States or by any State on account of race, color, or previous condition of servitude."

Any intelligent woman could see through the hypocrisy of the two amendments as they regarded women. The Fourteenth Amendment told them they were citizens, but left the states to make their election laws. The Fifteenth Amendment told the states what they could not do in their election laws, but left out the word "sex."

The problem of the best course to pursue after the ratification of these two amendments caused a great division in the woman suffrage movement which would keep it divided until 1890. One group was for bowing to the Fifteenth Amendment, and for fighting the suffrage battle state by state. After all, they had two victories behind them in Wyoming and Utah. The other faction maintained that the way to victory was by the passage of an amendment to the Federal Constitution. The state-by-staters formed the American Woman Suffrage Association. Those for the constitutional amendment became the National Woman Suffrage Association.

But during the next ten years, a number of personalities

and "isms" were to divide still further the suffrage front. Among them was a rash of new religious sects, the temperance movement, communal living, Spiritualism; and a controversial woman, Victoria Claflin Woodhull, depicted by her biographer, Emanie Sachs, as *The Terrible Siren.*

6 Woodhull for President

The signs on the fences and in the windows of the saloons
blazed out RE-ELECT OUR HERO — GRANT, or END
CORRUPTION WITH GREELEY. But the banners carried
by the marchers as they moved up Broadway on a frosty
October day in 1872 ignored the two opposing candidates
for the Presidency, and the tune played by their bands
was the campaign song of neither major political party.
Each time the drums rolled off, the bands played the tune
"Comin' thru the Rye," and the marchers, mostly women,
with a scattering of men, sang lustily:

> Hark the sound of women's voices
> Rising in their might.
> 'Tis the daughters of Columbia,
> Pleading for their right.
> Flock around Victoria's banner,
> Wave the signal still.
> Brothers, let us share your freedom,
> Help us and we will.
> See emblazoned on our standard
> Words of purest gold,

> Womankind shall not be fettered
> Nor her birthright sold.
> Never yield to rank injustice;
> Alter evil laws.
> Brothers, won't you stand beside us,
> In our righteous cause?

The banners waved in the autumn sunlight proclaiming VICTORY WITH VICTORIA, WOODHULL AND DOUGLASS, and VICTORIA WOODHULL FOR PRESIDENT. Near the head of the parade, riding in an open carriage drawn by four sleek black horses, was a strikingly beautiful woman. Beside her, with his tall silk hat in his lap, sat a tall, dignified Negro. The riders were Victoria Woodhull, the first woman candidate for President of the United States, and the distinguished Negro orator, Frederick Douglass, candidate for Vice President.

What Douglass was thinking that day as he rode up Broadway is hard to fathom. He had become the symbol, of the dignity, intelligence, and potentiality of the Negro people. His high standards of oratory and his command of language packed halls wherever he spoke. And now he was a candidate for Vice President on the Woodhull ticket, and riding beside the most controversial, notorious woman in America. The campaign and its outcome were a farce, and certainly did not add to Douglass's stature. Perhaps he was still repaying a debt to the women Abolitionists. Perhaps he realized that he was being "used."

Children were whipped for playing with the Claflin girls, and the people of Homer, Ohio, in 1845 called the Claflins "gutter folk." But although Victoria and Tennessee Claflin were poor, they were proud. Victoria believed that she was as divinely inspired as any Old Testament prophet. When eleven years old, she was sitting on the porch one day when some children came and peeked through the picket fence to see what a Claflin looked like. Victoria rose and shouted, "Let's go up to the Mount of Olives and I will preach to you." Out of curiosity, the children followed her to the top of a mound in back of the Claflin house. First, Victoria prayed earnestly for their sins. Then she noticed that they were getting bored, so she told them a story about three Indians scalping settlers. Throughout her life, Victoria could always "feel" an audience.

Even at the age of eleven, Victoria Claflin claimed to be conversing with the spirit world. The year before, when she was baby-sitting with a sick child, she said that two angels came into the sickroom and pushed her away from the bed. They fanned the child's fevered cheeks with their hands, and immediately the child was well. But her most important "vision" came shortly thereafter. A tall stately figure, dressed in a Greek tunic, whom Victoria later called "Demosthenes," came to her and promised that she would grow rich, own a luxurious mansion in a great seaport city, and would become the ruler of her country. "Demosthenes" was to be seventy-five per cent right, but spirits aren't always careful about election returns.

Tennessee Claflin, Victoria's younger sister, also claimed to have "satanic powers," and the children of Homer were afraid of her. She foretold a fire in the cupola of Dickinson Seminary, and pin-pointed the time of the fire so accurately that some people believed she set the fire. Again she stopped at a neighbor's house, and the housewife offered her some fruit. Tennessee asked, "Where did you put the best?" The woman blushed, because she had hidden the best fruit when she saw Tennessee coming. Soon "Buck" Claflin, Tennessee's father, in one of his frequent periods of unemployment, hung out a sign:

HAVE YOUR PAST READ AND YOUR FUTURE TOLD
T. Claflin
Fee — One Dollar

In the 1840's, religious revivals, Spiritualism, and other isms were the talk of Ohio. Tennessee and Victoria Claflin, now professional Spiritualists, and unconventional in their behavior, had been born into poverty and a miserable environment. Now, with their strange talents, they circulated among the many pseudo-intellectuals who were taking up various movements. Among the group was a young doctor, Canning Woodhull, and Victoria Claflin became Mrs. Woodhull in 1853, when she was only sixteen. It was a good marriage from Victoria's viewpoint. Woodhull was the son of a rich father, but he was an irresponsible playboy. Within a week, the marriage was on the rocks. Victoria said that Canning was an incurable alcoholic. Others said that Victoria drove him to drink.

After her divorce, Victoria drifted about the country as a seamstress in California, a cigar girl in Chicago, and as a part-time Spiritualist when she could find clients. Next she teamed up with Tennessee and toured the Midwest selling "Tennessee's Elixir," which was guaranteed to cure cancer, and holding Spiritualist seances where they made ouija boards write "spirit messages."

After a short stay in Chicago where the sisters operated a Magnetic Healing Infirmary, they moved to St. Louis where Victoria met Colonel James H. Blood. Colonel Blood commanded the Sixth Missouri Infantry during the Civil War, and was a sincere Spiritualist. He was also a mild socialist, and married. Soon, he temporarily dropped his last name, became James Harvey, left his wife, and went on tour with Victoria.

Two years later, "Demosthenes" in his purple tunic reappeared to Victoria during the night. This time he directed her to go to New York City, to a house at 17 Great Jones Street, which he said would be awaiting her. Victoria called Tennessee to join her, and with Colonel Blood took off for the metropolis.

At first, the going was rough. Victoria was now going in for faith healing, but clients were slow to come, and Colonel Blood couldn't find a job. Now the Greek Stranger made good another of his predictions. As Emanie Sachs put it in her biography, *The Terrible Siren,* "Commodore Vanderbilt had good reason to believe in miracles, he was one." Starting as a ferryboat captain at twenty-three, he owned sixty steamships by the time he was sixty-three. At seventy, he started buying up railroads, and was a financial monarch in New York. But although Commodore Vanderbilt did not go in for "magic mysteries" on Wall Street, he was soon practicing them at 17 Great Jones Street.

The Commodore had, or imagined he had, a number of ills, which doctors had not been able to cure, and he had made the rounds of the faith healers. Now he came to the Woodhull-Claflin Magnetic Healing Studio. They began magnetizing the Commodore regularly, and he liked it well enough to ask Tennessee to marry him, she said. But the Commodore was now seventy-five, and Tennessee didn't want to stop the flow of golden eggs by becoming the wife of the golden "goose". So she turned him down.

On January 20, 1870, the New York *Herald,* commenting on the disgraceful effrontery of the woman's rights movement, cited as an example the appearance of Woodhull, Claflin & Company on Wall Street. Three years later, Tennessee said that the firm had made $700,000. The Commodore's advice had been good.

The same year the Woodhull-Claflin brokerage house

opened its doors, Victoria met a strange philosopher, Stephen Andrews. He was highly educated, adept in a number of languages, and interested in everything, including woman's rights and Spiritualism. Colonel Blood was temporarily forgotten, but he remained loyal.

Victoria now developed an enormous appetite for respectability. With plenty of money in their tills, the sisters began publishing *Woodhull & Claflin's Weekly*, the first issue hitting the street on May 14, 1870.

Up in Boston, Julia Ward Howe was writing for the *Woman's Journal*, a conservative suffragist newspaper; and in New York State, Elizabeth Stanton was publishing *The Revolution*. Neither knew of Victoria Woodhull, and so neither could know that "Demosthenes," in his purple tunic, had appeared to Victoria and told her that she was ready to fulfil his last prediction. The next issue of *Woodhull & Claflin's Weekly* carried the headline: VICTORIA WOODHULL CANDIDATE FOR PRESIDENT OF THE UNITED STATES.

Immediately the stunned suffrage leaders began looking into Victoria's past and present. They found plenty, and soon Susan Anthony called on Victoria to tell her why the National Woman Suffrage Association couldn't work with her. Miss Anthony shouldn't have been surprised at the subsequent scorching blasts against her and her Association in the *Weekly*.

To launch her campaign, Victoria held a press conference in her beautiful home, predicted by "Demosthenes." She shocked reporters when she entered what she called her "Cinderella Room," wearing a knee-length, low-cut dress. After a sizzling silence, a reporter said, "But Mrs. Woodhull, if you appear on the street in that dress, the police will arrest you." Victoria replied, "No, they won't. When I am ready to make my appearance in this dress, no police-man will touch me. Presidents of the United States are not subject to arrest."

Now Victoria received a surprise visit from a surprising person, Benjamin F. Butler of Massachusetts. In a previous book, *Impeached!*, this author described Ben Butler as follows: "Searching the pages of history, including his own memoirs, it is impossible to find anyone who liked Benjamin Franklin Butler, unless it was his mother. . . . He was a short man with a little paunch. He grew a villainous, drooping mustache. One squinting eye peered straight ahead, while its twin enabled lawyer Butler to look both the judge and the jury straight in the eye at the same time." Butler had served in Congress, where he was one of the prosecutors at the impeachment trial of President Andrew Johnson. He was known as a crafty politician, and was notorious as a "sharp" lawyer.

Immediately, Butler was attracted by the charms of presidential candidate Woodhull. He said that he was in favor of woman suffrage, but didn't like Susan Anthony and her National Woman Suffrage Association. Was there anything he could do to help? he asked Victoria. Victoria told him of Susan Anthony's visit and that the Association wouldn't support her. Then the pair huddled and came out with a typical Butler maneuver, and Victoria was just the person to carry it out.

The National Woman Suffrage Convention was to have its annual convention in Washington, December 21, 1870. It was planned to pass resolutions which would be read to the House Judiciary Committee *following* the convention. During November and early December, Victoria souped-up her campaign, although the presidential election was almost two years hence. Woodhull-for-President badges were produced by the thousand. There were window cards, posters, banners, hatbands, and, of course, spreads in the *Weekly*.

Victoria Woodhull arrived in Washington via the morning train on December 21. While the delegates of the National Association were electing a permanent chairman, praying and listening to long addresses of welcome, Victoria Woodhull was speaking before a hearing of a charmed House Judiciary Committee — by arrangement of Benjamin F. Butler.

On the stage of the convention, a copy of the morning newspaper was being passed around by the convention officers. Susan Anthony hurriedly met with Isabella Beecher. Ben Butler had released the news that Victoria would appear before the Judiciary Committee in time for it to appear in the editions which the delegates would receive

On Dec. 21, 1870, beautiful Mrs. Woodhull delivered an eloquent address on woman's rights before the Judiciary Committee of the House of Representatives of the U.S.

in the morning. He had seen to it that the Associated Press was fully briefed. Now the convention passed a motion to recess until afternoon. "What can we do now?" the leaders asked. What they did was to hire carriages and race to the Capitol where Victoria was still charming the congressmen.

As Emanie Sachs described the scene: "She wore a plain dark dress with a blue necktie, her short brown hair curled under an Alpine hat. She looked so pale they wondered if she were going to faint. When she resumed reading, her voice trembled and broke. Suddenly her face flushed; it lighted; beauty gilded it. Her voice cleared, and gathered deep musical tones. Her grace, her engaging manner captivated every man and woman there. Her charm leaped out as if it had antennae."

That afternoon when the female dignitaries assembled on the convention platform, seated beside Susan B. Anthony were Victoria Woodhull and her sister, Tennessee. Ben Butler had told Victoria earlier, "It is only when they can't imitate it, that they complain of my sharpness."

When the afternoon session was called to order, Victoria was introduced to the delegates by Isabella Beecher Hooker, sister of Henry Ward Beecher. Again, Victoria played the shrinking violet. She apologized for her timidity, and gave a report on her conference with the Judiciary Committee. She told them that the representatives had assured her of a favorable report on her proposed suffrage bill, and that every man in the House was behind *her* in the suffrage movement.

For Victoria, the triumph was stunning. She had jumped the gun by getting to the Judiciary Committee before Susan Anthony, and she had been the first woman to speak in the Capitol and she had won the hearts of the politicians. She had snatched the spotlight from every feminist — Lucretia

Mott to Anna Dickinson. Furthermore, she had won their support and admiration. She had fired them to action instead of talk. Now at the end of the convention, they were talking of appearing at registration places in droves, demanding to be registered. The old leaders developed aggressiveness which they had never known before. Victoria for President — hooray!

The American Woman Suffrage Association, the moderate rival of the National, now shrieked at the latter for supporting such a "brazen hussy" as "that Woodhull woman." Men wrote letters to Elizabeth Stanton asking how she could support a woman with the morals of Mrs. Woodhull. But Miss Stanton, who had previously been shocked by Victoria's antics, now wrote to one of these men: "In regard to the gossip about Mrs. Woodhull, I have one answer — when the men who make the laws for us in Washington can stand forth and declare themselves pure and unspotted from the sins mentioned in the Decalogue, then we will demand that every woman who makes a constitutional argument on our platform, shall be as chaste as Diana. If our good men will only trouble themselves about the virtue of their own sex as they do about ours, if they will make one moral code for both men and women, we shall have a nobler type of womanhood."

The other woman suffrage leaders, who had shunned Victoria like a contagious disease, and who had gasped at her bold editorials in *Woodhull & Claflin's Weekly*, now fell over themselves to get on her campaign bandwagon. Again, Elizabeth Stanton wrote to retired Lucretia Mott: "I have thought much about Mrs. Woodhull, and have come to the conclusion that it is a great impertinence in any of us to pry into her personal affairs. This woman stands before us today as an able speaker and writer. Her face, manners and conversation all indicate the triumph of the moral, intellectual and spiritual."

Susan Anthony, completely charmed, said that Mrs. Woodhull's morals were as good as those of most congressmen. She went so far as to say that she would welcome all the infamous women in New York "if they would make speeches for freedom." And she wrote to Victoria, "Bravo! My dear Woodhull . . . Glorious old Ben (Butler)! He is surely going to pronounce the word that will settle the woman question, just as he did the word "contraband" that so summarily settled the Negro questions. . . . Go ahead doing — bright, glorious, young and strong in spirit."

Now Victoria hit the campaign trail. Her first appearances included the Mercantile Library Association of New York, the Cooper Union Institute, which had heard Lincoln, and the Labor Reform Convention — all in New York. Not confining herself to woman's rights, she aimed her speeches at labor and economics. Her speeches were written by Stephen Andrews (labor), Ben Butler (woman suffrage), Commodore Vanderbilt (economics) and Colonel Blood (everything else).

But now, some of Victoria's unconventional views were beginning to attract the attention of the nation's press and the anti-feminist male population. Furthermore, they concentrated on the rompings of Tennessee which were much better press.

The political year, 1871, opened auspiciously for Victoria. The hostile press was taking her seriously and attacking her bitterly. Her name was on the front page of every major newspaper. Horace Greeley, who in past years had given space in his *Tribune* to every radical cause, was now the Liberal Republican candidate for President, and he editorially attacked all that Victoria Woodhull espoused, including woman suffrage.

Governor Hawley of Connecticut wrote a guest editorial in the Hartford *Courant*: "We have hesitated whether to advertise a certain disreputable weekly journal in New York, which is edited by a woman, by denouncing its real character. It becomes however a duty to do it, when we see that the journal is read by woman Spiritists and woman Suffragists, who may shut their eyes to its immorality, and who introduce it into respectable households where there are virtuous girls. . . ." No Madison Avenue public relations firm of the 1960's could have done for Victoria Woodhull what she and the *Weekly* were doing for herself. Her publicity nearly equaled that of Grant and Greeley.

Now Victoria got down to solid politics. She marched into a registration place, accompanied by reporters, and demanded to be placed on the voting list. Of course, she was refused, but hundreds of woman suffrage supporters followed her example. Then Tennessee got into the act and announced her candidacy for Congress from the Eighth New York District. Next came the Victoria League, the new political party that officially was to nominate Victoria for the Presidency. Theodore Tilton, an ace magazine writer, moved into the "Demosthenes house" to write Victoria's campaign biography.

With nearly all of the more aggressive woman suffrage leaders solidly behind her, Victoria now concentrated on the labor vote. Her articles, undoubtedly ghost-written by Colonel Blood or Theodore Tilton, appeared in the *American Workman*. She was perhaps the first Presidential candidate to distribute autographed photographs widely, and in later years, historians of the American labor movement reported

Victoria Claflin Woodhull, who wanted to be President of the United States, asserting her right to vote.

finding glamorous photographs of Victoria in the home of every old-time labor leader.

Although Victoria's campaign speeches were usually of a high order, and while her rallies throughout the East and Midwest were jammed to suffocation, her name could not be disassociated from her notorious reputation. And unfortunately, unlike Lucy Stone, Elizabeth Stanton and Susan Anthony, she could not cope with hecklers. When heckled, she lost control of herself and fought back, making matters worse.

Election Day, 1872, came, but there is no record of how many votes were cast for Victoria Woodhull. There couldn't be, because she had not bothered to have presidential electors nominated in any state. "Demosthenes" should have told her about that. Victoria and Tennessee spent the day in the Ludlow Street jail on a charge of publishing obscene literature in *Woodhull & Claflin's Weekly*. For months Victoria's financial position had been declining. Her campaign expenses, spread over two years, had been huge. The social reforms which she advocated had alienated Commodore Vanderbilt and her other Wall Street supporters. In the last months of the campaign, Theodore Tilton deserted her to support Horace Greeley, who was trounced by Grant. Frederick Douglass had been of little help.

Victoria was not invited to the next annual meeting of the National Woman Suffrage Association, although Susan Anthony continued to defend her. After a few years of lecturing, becoming more controversial than ever, Victoria Woodhull moved to England, married a wealthy gentleman (she had never married Colonel Blood), and lived a quiet, useful life until her death in 1927. But from the day her *Weekly* announced Victoria Woodhull as candidate for President, the woman suffrage movement was never the same again.

7 *The Test Case*

It was 1875, and the scene in the chamber of the United States Supreme Court was as dull as it always had been and has been ever since. The justices in their silk robes were thoroughly bored by the droning pleas of the attorneys for the plaintiff and the defendant. When the pleas, which seemed interminable, came to an end, the justices quietly retired — to study the case of *Minor versus Happerset.*

Few people aside from constitutional lawyers have ever read or heard of the *Minor versus Happerset* decision, or its background. But President Lyndon Johnson knew it very well when he sent his voter registration bill to Congress to enable more than two per cent of Alabama's Negroes to enter a polling place. The Supreme Court's decision in the case of *Minor versus Happersett* was the basis upon which Alabama had drafted its literacy test law for voting eligibility. Until President Johnson's bill was passed by Congress, Alabama could rely on *Minor versus Happersett* to defend a literacy test for Negroes which a university graduate might not be able to pass.

Although volumes have been written about the heroines

of woman suffrage, this author had to appeal to Missouri's current attorney general, Norman H. Anderson, to find out Mrs. Minor's first name and the background of the case. According to Attorney General Anderson, the lady was Virginia L. Minor. Her husband, Francis Minor, was a lawyer, and a man of some wealth.

During the 1872 election campaign, Virginia Minor, following the example set by Victoria Woodhull, appeared before a registration officer, Reese Happersett, and demanded that her name be entered on the voting list. In demanding her right to vote, she cited the Fourteenth Amendment. Reese Happersett referred to the constitution and laws of the State of Missouri which barred women from registering as voters. Unlike Victoria Woodhull and hundreds of other women, who appeared at registration places merely as a demonstration and then accepted the decision of the officials, Virginia Minor did something about it.

A few months later, Mrs. Minor, with Francis Minor as her attorney and co-plaintiff, sued Reese Happersett in the St. Louis Circuit Court. The Minors, of course, lost their case, and immediately appealed to the Supreme Court of Missouri. Again the plea was that Reese Happersett had violated the Fourteenth Amendment to the Constitution of the United States, and that the Circuit Court of St. Louis was "in error."

Judge Vories of the Missouri Supreme Court stated the case: "This was an action brought in the St. Louis Circuit Court by husband and wife against the defendant, who was a registering officer, for refusing to register Virginia L. Minor, the wife, as a lawful voter." With alacrity the State Supreme Court upheld the decision of the Circuit Court, and Chief Justice Vories commented: "The plaintiff is a native-born, free, white citizen of the United States and of the State of Missouri . . . and she possesses the qualifications of an elector in all respects, *except as to the matter of sex* [italics added]."

The decision came as no surprise to Attorney Minor. He actually welcomed it, because it would give him the opportunity to do what no Negro, state government, or woman had done, test the Fourteenth Amendment to the Federal Constitution. Mrs. Minor and her husband appealed to the U.S. Supreme Court. The case was placed on the Court's calendar for the 1875 term.

The arguments for the plaintiff and the defendant were no different from those entered in Missouri, except for length. The plaintiff's attorneys argued that each state had a right to determine qualifications for voting. Francis Minor and his law partner argued that Virginia was a citizen and therefore entitled to vote under the Fourteenth Amendment.

A few days after the hearing, the Supreme Court justices returned to their chamber. The Court's decision in the case of *Minor versus Happersett* was short, as Supreme Court decisions go, only a bit over eight pages. But it served to focus the attention of woman's rights leaders on their one great problem, the status of state election laws, just as President Lyndon Johnson focused the attention of the nation on literacy tests as prerequisites for voting.

The decision, which was unanimous, was read by Chief Justice Morrison R. Waite of Ohio. First, he reviewed Mrs. Minor's appeal which asked the Court to find the Missouri suffrage law unconstitutional, and that the question before the Court was whether, since the adoption of the Fourteenth Amendment, a woman who is a citizen of the United States and the State of Missouri is a voter in that state, notwithstanding the laws of that state which "confine the right of suffrage to men alone."

But then Chief Justice Waite "lowered the boom." He said: "The United States has no voters in the states of its own creation. The elective officers of the United States are all elected directly or indirectly by state voters." Then he touched upon a point which had been a bone of contention since the Declaration of Independence: "We find that in no state were all citizens permitted to vote." Here the Chief Justice was referring chiefly to the property qualifications for voting which had existed at one time or another in most states. There had been a firm belief among conservative citizens that only those who paid substantial taxes should be allowed to vote. In many states, the person who owned no property was barred from voting.

Chief Justice Waite then turned to that section of the Constitution which guarantees a republican form of government in each state, but he reflected that the Constitution did not define what was republican, and therefore "it could not be claimed that a state did not have a republican form of government because it did not let women vote." In emphasizing that states control their own election laws, the Chief Justice cited Missouri, Alabama, Arkansas, Florida, Georgia, and several other states where, under certain conditions, foreigners were allowed to vote provided they had declared their intentions of becoming citizens.

Chief Justice Waite then concluded: "Being unanimously of the opinion that the Constitution of the United States does not confer the right of suffrage upon anyone, and that the constitutions and laws of the several states which commit that important trust to man alone are not necessarily void, we affirm the judgment of the Missouri Supreme Court."

And so ended the almost forgotten case of *Minor versus Happersett*. But Virginia L. Minor was remembered for many years by the suffragists. She had lost her case, but she had done something very important. She had demanded her right to vote through the courts rather than the soapbox. She had clarified the course to woman suffrage. Yes, there would have to be parades, speeches, agitation, and the support of the press. But all the women in every state would never be able to vote until the Supreme Court could no longer say "no."

With the decision of the Supreme Court, Virginia Minor became a national heroine of the suffrage movement. Little known before outside her home state, she was annually a speaker at the National Woman Suffrage conventions, and she was booked for speaking tours throughout the country.

Having had her plea rejected by the highest court of the land, it is natural that she believed in obtaining the ballot for women by constitutional amendment, and she couldn't go along with Lucy Stone's state-by-state theory. Nevertheless, whenever a woman suffrage amendment was on a referendum ballot in any state, Virginia Minor was usually there.

8 *The Spirit of '76*

The suffrage leaders came out of the Woodhull-for-President campaign with many scars. Now their opponents would charge them unjustly with favoring Victoria's ideas. Victoria's morals and her public rantings made her the opposition symbol of what could be expected from a woman candidate for office. Because they had to defend her, the prestige of leaders Anthony and Stanton certainly was not enhanced. And the antics of Tennessee, Victoria's sister, caused men to nod their heads and say, "She is a typical suffragist."

But the women had learned more than they realized from the Woodhull campaign. They came to realize that there was more to winning the vote than holding windy annual conventions in Washington, petitioning congressmen and appearing at occasional legislative hearings. Victoria, beating them to the hearing of the House Judiciary Committee, taught them that slick political strategy is sometimes necessary. Victoria taught them the value of publishing a newspaper. She taught them how to campaign and draw crowds; that it was necessary to get outside the Northeast and really "stump the country." Yes, the suffrage movement was never the same after that Woodhull-for-President year.

The feminists also learned a lesson from the women of Wyoming. Here was a territory which the suffrage leaders had ignored, the first state where women obtained the franchise. The National and the American associations must have been rather shamefaced to observe women voting without their leadership. They probably made a serious assessment of the Wyoming victory, and they must have come up with the observation that men voted women the franchise in Wyoming because they believed that the state would be morally cleaner if women had an influence in the government. The decent men realized that they needed the women to get rid of a very bad situation. Wyoming had given the suffrage leaders a new and potent slogan: *America will be a better place to live in when women go to the polls.*

The year 1876 was to be a gala year, the centennial of the Declaration of Independence, and the women planned to make the most of it. The Centennial Year was to mark a hundred years of freedom for American males, and the suffragists planned to remind the men that women still had few rights, and those rights had only recently been obtained in three or four states.

In the summer of 1876, there was to be America's first great international world's fair, the Philadelphia Exposition. The Liberty Bell would be on display, and so would the suffragists. There was a huddle of the high command — Anna Dickinson, Lucy Stone, Stanton, Anthony, Isabella Beecher Hooker, and a new recruit, Attorney Belva Lockwood.

The result of their plotting was something new to the movement, something more akin to la Woodhull than Lucretia Mott. At Philadelphia they would assemble all of

A new recruit to the suffrage cause in 1876, woman lawyer Belva Lockwood was to campaign devotedly for over forty years.

their leaders and as many followers as possible. They would attract attention to their cause by controversial methods: parades, propaganda, demonstrations, unexpected rallies, and most of the basic elements of Martin Luther King's nonviolent tactics. They would rent space at the Exposition and use it as a propaganda base. They would pay the rent by the sale of suffragist literature, badges, and souvenirs. They would use the fair to sell suffrage, just as Alexander Graham Bell would use it to sell the telephone.

Eighteen seventy-six was more than the Centennial Year, it was also a presidential election year; and for the first time, the National Association, favoring a federal constitutional amendment, would put pressure on the two major party conventions.

After a preliminary convention in New York, the National Woman Suffrage Association moved on Philadelphia. First, they attempted to rent Carpenter's Hall, the seat of the Continental Congress, for their headquarters, and were refused, as doubtless they expected to be. Then they rented spacious rooms on Chestnut Street. From the Chestnut Street base, a flood of suffrage literature was mailed, plus letters to the delegates of the Republican and Democratic national conventions, urging a woman suffrage plank in their respective platforms. There were letters blasting the Supreme Court for the *Minor versus Happersett* decision.

The Philadelphia Exposition was to open on July 4, with great ceremony. Most of the nation's dignitaries and many European heads of state would sit on the stage in front of Independence Hall. On the ground that she represented half of the population of the United States, with which Lucy Stone would hardly agree, Susan Anthony wrote to General Hawley, chairman of the centennial commission, asking that women be represented on the platform. General Hawley replied that he had already assigned all of the seats, and could make no changes. Next Miss Anthony asked for a place on the program to read her Woman's Declaration of Independence. The program had already been set, General Hawley said. Of course, Miss Anthony had known the answers to her requests before she made them.

The Glorious Fourth arrived and the opening of the Centennial Year. On the platform in front of Independence

Hall were seated Dom Pedro, Emperor of Brazil; Count Rochembeau of France; Prince Oscar of Sweden; the commissioners of Russia, Austria, Spain, Prussia, Great Britain, Turkey; and Acting Vice President Wheeler. To Centennial commissioner Hawley, the arrangements had gone off perfectly. Everything seemed under control. But he would soon regret one concession he had made. After rebuffing Susan Anthony for a place on the platform, he had broken down and allotted the National Woman Suffrage Association fifty reserved seats in the audience.

The band which had been playing during the entrance of the notables now played "The Star Spangled Banner," and the Centennial Year had begun. General Hawley stepped forward and introduced Acting Vice President Wheeler. Wheeler came forward — and so did Susan Anthony. Climbing to the platform, she presented the Acting Vice President with a parchment copy of the Woman's Declaration of Independence. Wheeler, taken by surprise, accepted the document and mumbled something which history has not recorded. General Hawley was turning a slightly pale green while Miss Anthony, without a word, left the platform.

But while Miss Anthony was making her silent presentation, the other forty-nine women were passing out copies of the Declaration. The meeting was in a state of pandemonium. Men were standing on their chairs, many demanding copies of the Declaration, and the Emperor of Brazil looked extremely confused. General Hawley was shouting for order, and he got it only after Miss Anthony dramatically led her women out of the meeting, followed by a considerable part of the audience, to the bandstand which had just been vacated by the musicians. There, just outside

the exposition grounds, the suffragists led the most successful and noisiest rally in the history of the movement up to
that time. Yes, they had learned a lot from Victoria Woodhull.

Following the demonstration in Philadelphia, the National
Association introduced its first newspaper, *The Ballot Box*,
for nationwide circulation, published in Toledo, Ohio, by
Sarah Langdon Williams. It was fruitlessly distributed at
the Democratic and Republican national conventions where
the delegates refused even to vote on a woman suffrage
plank. But it was read, and an increasing number of
leaders of both parties were declared in favor of the proposed Sixteenth Amendment, which had been drafted by
Susan Anthony, and which contained the exact wording of
the eventual Nineteenth. Among these were Representatives Banks of Massachusetts, Henry Blair of New Hampshire, John Serman of Ohio (brother of William Tecumseh),
Mitchell of Oregon, and Freylinghuysen of New Jersey —
all influential members of Congress.

Now, after two years of laying solid groundwork, begun
at the Philadelphia Exposition, after petitions to Congress
and the state legislatures, and with a hard core of congressmen dedicated to woman suffrage, on January 10, 1878,
Senator A. A. Sargent of California rose in the Senate and
introduced the Sixteenth Amendment to the Constitution.
The Committee on Privileges and Elections immediately
granted hearings to the National Association on January 11
and 12. The first hearing was opened by the reading of a
statement by Victor Hugo, the famous French author of
Les Misérables. Hugo wrote: "Our ill-balanced society
seems as if it would take from woman all that nature has
endowed her with. Man has had his law; he has made it

himself. Woman has only the law of man. She is by this law civilly a minor and morally a slave. Her education is embued with this twofold character of inferiority. There must be reform here to the benefit of civilization, truth and light."

Next came the reading of a statement by the highly respected British philosopher and member of Parliament, John Stuart Mill. His statement said in part, "The legal subordination of one sex to another is wrong in itself, and now one of the chief hindrances to human improvement. No slave is a slave to the same extent a woman is." On woman's eligibility for voting, he continued, "With equality of experience and general faculties, a woman sees much more than a man of what is immediately before her."

Now with women voting for all territorial offices in Wyoming and Utah, and for school committees in a number of other states, Elizabeth Stanton hammered away at the inconsistencies in a woman's rights if she moved from one state to another. If she were competent to vote for governor in Wyoming, why not if she moved to New York? If she could be tried by a jury including women in Wyoming, why was she not entitled to her constitutional right to be tried by a jury of her peers in Pennsylvania? If she could run for school committee in Massachusetts, why did she not have the same right in Maryland? Not to have equal rights in all states was a defiance of the intent of the Constitution, she said.

After the two days of the hearings, the Washington *Evening Star* editorialized: "It is noticed that the opponents of woman suffrage are coming more and more to be based on expediency, and hardly attempt to answer the claim that as American citizens women are entitled to the right. . . . But woman suffrage must become a matter of policy for a political party before it can be realized." And the *Evening Star* was so right.

But now the suffrage leaders ran into an impediment which was to plague them until 1920 — their own sex. During the week following the Senate hearing, a group of women arrived in Washington representing an organization which had been founded in 1871, the Anti-Suffrage Society. Among its officers in 1878 were the wives of Admiral Dahlgren and General William T. Sherman. That week, Mrs. Dahlgren appeared before the Senate Committee to speak against the proposed Sixteenth Amendment. Her argument was the fifty-year-old wail about the sanctity of the family. She said, "When women ask for a distinct political life, a separate vote, they forget or they willingly ignore the higher law, whose logic may be thus condensed: Marriage is a sacred unity. Each family is represented by its head just as the State ultimately finds the same unity through a series of representations. Out of this comes peace, concord, proper representation and adjustment — union. The new doctrine, which is illusive, may be thus defined: Marriage is a mere compact, and means diversity. Each family therefore must have a separate individual representation, out of which rises diversity or division, and discord becomes the cornerstone of the State."

The Senate Committee on Privileges and Elections turned in an adverse report on the proposed Sixteenth Amendment, and it was buried in the Senate by "laying it on the table." But while the Senate hearings were going on, the House of Representatives, by a vote of 169 to 87, passed a bill to permit women attorneys to practice before the Supreme Court. Attorney Belva Lockwood immediately took the oath.

The burial of the proposed Sixteenth Amendment was

hard to bear, it had seemed to have a chance of passage. Another amendment couldn't be introduced until after the presidential election of 1880. Now the leaders of the National Association surveyed the wreckage. Whether they saw what we can see today, they have not told us, but if they did, this was what they would have recognized: that the women of America were hopelessly divided into four categories. There was the National Association whose only goal was to obtain the passage and ratification of a woman suffrage amendment to the Constitution. Then there was the American Association which was battling for women's rights, state by state. It didn't fight for the franchise until other legal rights had been won. Susan Anthony of the National was for holding huge conventions, employing the nation's best speakers and petitioning congressmen. But Lucy Stone, "the loner," was appearing before state legislatures, city councils, tax commissions and school committees. And ·inch by inch, Lucy Stone was winning her battle.

Lucy could be spectacular, too, in her own quiet way. She had allowed her New York City home to be "sold for taxes," because she refused to submit to taxation without representation. She didn't make a speech about it, but the incident received ample coverage in the New York press. In state after state, Lucy Stone was obtaining legislation which gave women some degree of legal rights, and sometimes the right to vote for certain offices. Unfortunately, up to this point, there had been no joint meetings or communication between the two major woman suffrage organizations.

Then there was the third category of American women, the Anti-Suffrage Society, composed of the wives of prominent men, many of whom were Civil War generals, and their voices had a strong influence on Congress, especially when they pounded away with the same time-worn arguments of their husbands.

But by far the greatest impediment to ballots for women was the vast majority of American women who *just didn't care*. They were totally indifferent, and many of them would remain so until after 1920. They would never become aroused until politicians needed their vote, and then they would have to be dragged to the polls.

In the gloom after the burial of the proposed Sixteenth Amendment there suddenly burst forth a bright light in the form of a dramatically shocking, yet exciting *cause célèbre*. There would be others, but this one served best to illuminate the disparity between men and women in America. And this brings us back to that gruff, unpolished politician, Senator Ben Wade of Ohio. Ben Wade was the last person anyone would suspect of being a feminist. He wouldn't have admitted it if anyone had asked him. He had fought his way up the political ladder by Neanderthal tactics from justice of the peace to his election to the U.S. Senate in 1851. As president *Pro Tempore* of the Senate after Lincoln's assassination, according to the Presidential Succession Act of the time, he was within a heartbeat of the White House during Andrew Johnson's administration, and with typical Wade sensitivity had not seen fit to abstain from voting in the impeachment trial of Andrew Johnson. He saw no reason for not trying to vote himself into the White House. But as incongruous as it seems, by 1878, Ben Wade had become, along with mild, gentlemanly Senator Henry Blair of New Hampshire, the spearhead for woman suffrage in the Senate. Like his former colleague in Congress, Ben Butler, Wade would not make his fight by moralistic pleading. He lacked Butler's cunning, and seemed somewhat of a bull in the legislative china shop, but his approach was the jolt, and jolt the Senate he did.

For his legislative bomb, he had the story of Anna Carroll! There wasn't a scrap of paper in Wade's possession which contained a reference to the story. It had been one of the few completely hidden military secrets of the War. But Wade had an outline of Anna Carroll's plan. The government archives had the original plans, and Wade had memoranda between Secretary Stanton and himself. They all dovetailed. Now Ben Wade was ready to "blow."

After the proposed Sixteenth Amendment was tabled indefinitely, Wade rose in the Senate for a good, long talk. He told the whole story of Anna Carroll to an astounded Senate and press gallery. He explained the necessity for extreme secrecy; that he was the only living person possessing the secret, and then he presented documentation which no one but five persons had ever seen, and he was the only surviving member of the five.

Further, he revealed that for her brilliant strategy, which had started turning defeats into victories for the North, which eventually led to the fall of Atlanta and Vicksburg, Anna Carroll had not received one penny from the War Department. Because of the secrecy involved, she had not even received a letter of thanks from President Lincoln. After the War and Lincoln's assassination, neither former Secretary Stanton nor Wade had ever told the story to Andrew Johnson.

Then Wade told the Senate that Anna Carroll, although of an artistocratic Maryland family, was in financial straits. He offered a Senate resolution, to be delivered to the House, where all money bills must originate, that a bill be initiated to pay Anna Carroll $10,000. Little enough, he said. But an economy-minded Senate refused to pass the resolution.

Now the suffrage leaders had something to scream about in the press. Not only had Anna Carroll been wronged by the government, but here was a woman who had devised a master plan of strategy, who could not vote, while Generals Grant and Sherman, and every Yankee soldier who carried a rifle in the Tennessee campaign had the ballot. At the same time, they could point to Belva Lockwood, a seasoned authority on constitutional law and practicing before the Supreme Court, unable to vote, while any small-town, self-made lawyer could vote and hold office.

There was another star in the gloom which cast its beam from Europe and gave the sign: "Woman suffrage is inevitable." In Great Britain, a woman suffrage bill had been debated in the House of Commons as early as 1867, with John Stuart Mill pressing for its passage, and although it was defeated, some 259 Englishwomen were placed on the voting rolls that year by local registrars. By 1869, many English women were voting in local elections. By 1878, suffrage bills were being defeated by only hairline margins. After all, the British male opposing woman suffrage, had two strikes on him to start with. On the British throne sat Queen Victoria, and she had been sitting there since 1837. Few British males could argue that Queen Victoria was not competent to hold public office while managing an empire on which the sun never set.

In France, the International Woman's Rights Congress convened in 1878 with delegates from France, Switzerland, Italy, Holland, and the United States. The French delegation included two senators, five deputies (equivalent to congressmen), and three Paris municipal councilors (all male). From Italy came a member of the national legislature and the Countess of Travers. Julia Ward Howe represented the United States. Anna Maria Mozzoni of

Milan, Italy, along with Mrs. Howe were the principal speakers. Victor Hugo, the French literary giant, presided over most of the sessions. At the climax of the International Congress, the delegates rose and sang Julia Howe's "Battle Hymn" — "As we go marching on." And marching they were, toward an elusive but inevitable victory.

9 *Becalmed*

It was the calm before the storm, an agonizingly long
calm — the period from the 1880's to the turn of the century.
It seemed to the leaders that there was just no progress at
the national level, and they were getting old and tired.

Every year saw the same seemingly hopeless routine.
The convention met and passed resolutions which were
delivered to members of Congress. At every session of Congress, Susan Anthony and Elizabeth Stanton appeared before the Judiciary Committees of both Houses to argue for
the proposed Sixteenth Amendment.

But Congress had developed a technique for disposing
of woman suffrage legislation, without coming out in the
open to oppose it. It was simple and it always worked.
Congress had foreseen that the ladies would become a
nuisance, but that it would seem ungentlemanly just to
turn them away. So at each session, some representative or
senator arose and introduced the Sixteenth Amendment.
Then the House referred the resolution to its Judiciary
Committee, and the Senate sent the resolution to its newly
acquired Committee on Woman Suffrage.

When the National Convention met, its representatives were politely received at the committee hearings. While the convention was still in session, the proposed Sixteenth Amendment was reported out of committee. Then it was immediately referred to the Judiciary Committees of both Houses for final consideration. This swift action was encouraging to lady delegates who went home with hope in their hearts. But then the committees either submitted an unfavorable report or just forgot about the whole thing. Thus woman suffrage never came to a showdown vote.

Susan Anthony had been in the crusade long enough to be a realist as well as an idealist. Had she been only a realist, she would have given up the fight long ago. She faced the fact that, except for the Civil War amendments, the Constitution hadn't been changed since 1804. To obtain two thirds of both Houses to make another basic change was hopeless at the time, and even if a woman suffrage amendment passed Congress, it could not be ratified by two thirds of the states.

Susan Anthony also faced the fact that the great majority of American women didn't care whether they had suffrage or not. When governors and senators taunted her, saying, "The women don't want to vote," she replied, "How do you know, have you asked them?" But down in her heart, she knew they were partly right.

Miss Anthony fully recognized that in the liquor lobby she faced her most powerful opponent. It was the most potent influence on government — national, state, and local. It made huge contributions to the campaign funds of both parties. It paid millions of dollars in taxes to states, municipalities, and the federal government. It bought the farmer's grain and corn. Making barrels and blowing bottles for the liquor trade were just two of the many industries that depended on liquor. Newspapers heavily relied on liquor advertising, railroads shipped carloads of beer, and hundreds of thousands of men and women were employed in the distilleries and breweries. The wings of the railroad lobby were beginning to be clipped, but from 1880 to 1917, politicians of both major political parties were polite to "Big Liquor." To the latter, woman suffrage meant Prohibition.

Another sober problem facing Susan Anthony was an aging leadership. She was in her seventies. Elizabeth Stanton was becoming more feeble, and Miss Anthony knew that her friendly competitor-colleague, Lucy Stone, would not be able to exercise her leadership much longer. Miss Anthony was tired, but still determined. There must be new blood, and soon.

But for those who let the trees obscure the forest, there was much that they didn't see, the evidence in so many places that the calm was about to erupt into a surge for woman suffrage. Perhaps it was clearer to pretty, restrained, eloquent, determined Lucy Stone. There is every indication that of the two leaders, she had the most comprehensive view of the national situation, by keeping an ever-vigilant eye on the state legislatures and city governments.

Colorado and Idaho had joined Wyoming and Utah in giving women full voting rights. In those four states women were voting for governors, congressmen, and presidential electors. Women had some limited degree of voting rights in half of the states, mostly in school district elections. Even conservative Louisiana permitted women who paid property taxes to vote in local or state referendums, when special appropriations were on the ballot. Women were holding political appointive offices: they were superintendents of schools, postmasters, justices of the peace, and police matrons. They were serving on boards of trustees of state colleges, state commissions on institutions, and health departments.

Another bright spot on the woman suffrage horizon was across the Atlantic. Women had the franchise in Ireland, although few went to the polls. Local suffrage was winning in England, and woman suffrage bills in Parliament were losing by ever-shrinking margins. In France, an effective woman's rights movement was being piloted by Alexandre Dumas and Victor Hugo. The crusade was advancing in Germany, Spain, Italy, and Sweden.

But two positive features of the suffragist campaign stand out before all of the others. One was an event, the other a woman. In December, 1890, the National Woman Suffrage Association met together for the first time with the American Association. Why it had not happened before is incredible. There never had been any animosity or rivalry between the two organizations. In fact, Susan Anthony and Lucy Stone admired each other. The National had concentrated on a constitutional amendment, while the American focused on the precinct, the city council and the state legislature. Both approaches were essential to woman suffrage, but for forty years the American and the National had been going their separate ways.

Perhaps an aging, weary, more contemplative Susan Anthony was seeing a more realistic picture. After receiving her annual run-around in the Senate and House Judiciary Committees, she began to realize that the situation in Congress would not improve until women, voting in the states, could exert pressure on their congressional representatives. Perhaps it was easier to amend state constitutions than the federal. Perhaps the steadily increasing vote for the proposed Sixteenth Amendment was due to Lucy Stone's work in the states. And so in 1890, Lucy Stone and Susan Anthony stood together on the stage of Washington's Lincoln Auditorium and received the cheers of their new organization, the National American Woman Suffrage Association.

It is possible, to some degree, to assess the impetus which this fusion gave to the suffrage cause. On the record, Lucy Stone had accomplished the most. She had built from the bottom: property rights, family rights, legal rights, improved working laws, and school district elections. Lucy and her workers were able to convince some business men that a woman paying taxes on an estate of $200,000 should have something to say about how her taxes were spent. Working rather quietly within a somewhat loose national organization, Lucy Stone did not become involved with Spiritualism, the Anti-Saloon League, and other controversial movements. But that was possibly one drawback. Lucy Stone's American Association didn't make headlines, whereas Susan Anthony's National did.

It was the great showman, P. T. Barnum, who once said to a reporter, "I don't care what you say about me as long as you spell my name right." Ever since the Seneca Falls convention, Susan Anthony and Elizabeth Stanton had been in the headlines, for better or for worse. Even the Woodhull-for-President campaign, although it made some laugh and others angry, brought reams of publicity. Horace Greeley's New York *Tribune*, although not supporting woman suffrage editorially, gave full coverage of the annual National conventions. In those days, metropolitan newspapers had wide circulation in rural areas, and Susan

Another 1890 newcomer, Carrie Chapman Catt, whose aggresive leadership carried the suffragists to victory in 1920.

Anthony, through the activities of the National Association, kept the woman suffrage cause constantly before reading America.

The merged convention of the American and National

Associations was the last great victory for both Susan Anthony and Lucy Stone. Lucy Stone was to die in 1894, and Susan Anthony would retire in 1900. Elizabeth Stanton had already retired. These three women, and Lucretia Mott before her death, had sustained and advanced the cause of woman suffrage since 1840.

Susan Anthony had realized for several years that new blood was needed in the movement, and she had the transfusion ready in the person of Carrie Chapman Catt. Miss Anthony firmly believed that victory would be won in the early part of the twentieth century. She wouldn't win it, but she wanted a woman to succeed her who would be thoroughly tried in battle.

Chapman Catt, as she prefered to be called, first appeared in the national limelight of woman suffrage at the National American convention of 1890, along with another woman who was to become a leader in the merged association, Alice Stone Blackwell, Lucy's daughter. Mrs. Catt had been selected as one of the principal speakers by Susan Anthony. On the platform, in her mid-thirties, she appeared vivacious, attractive and tough. Her maiden speech was a hard-hitting, straight-from-the-shoulder lesson in practical politics and organization, and that was to be her role in the woman suffrage movement, from that day to victory in 1920.

Mrs. Chapman Catt was on the platform again at the 1892 convention, but since her first national convention she had done a lot of homework, mostly done away from home. She had made a tour of the country to become fully informed on every phase of the suffragist movement. She had visited state leaders to question them on their multitude of problems. She had made charts of state organizations. She had analyzed the roll calls of state legislatures on woman

Alice Stone Blackwell, daughter of pioneer Lucy Stone, stepped forward at the 1890 convention to carry on the family crusade.

suffrage constitutional amendments. Perhaps most important, Mrs. Catt had sat down with women who, without the vote, were already working on county political party committees.

Home at last, Mrs. Catt analyzed her notes. These were her conclusions: The state organizations were too loosely knit and did not follow a uniform pattern; there was too much time spent in talk and tea, and not enough in political organizing; women in Utah, Wyoming, Colorado, and Idaho, who held political offices, should be used to effect in other states. At the national level, she thought, there were two great weaknesses. Since Garfield was a candidate for the Presidency, no suffrage leader had interviewed a President or a candidate to seek his support. It probably would have been fruitless, but at least he should have been "put on the spot."

But the greatest weakness, Mrs. Chapman Catt observed, had been the complete failure at the national conventions of the Democrats and Republicans. She believed that woman suffrage would never become a national issue until it got into the platform of one of the two major parties. But how to get it there? The Democratic National Committee had been downright rude. The Republicans had put on an appearance of more courtesy. They admitted the suffragist leaders into the platform committee room and let them speak for *as long as five minutes.* Then the platform committee just forgot about the whole thing. Mrs. Catt saw that the siutation would never improve until pressure was put on the convention delegates *at home.*

At the convention of 1895, Mrs. Catt made her first preliminary report, and it was not entirely appreciated by Susan Anthony. She said: "The great need of the hour is organization. There can be no doubt that the advocates of woman suffrage are to be numbered by millions, but it is a lamentable fact that our organization can count its numbers only by thousands. The reason for this condition is plain; the chief work of the suffragists for the past forty years has. been education and agitation, and not organization. The time has come when the educational work has borne its fruit, and there are states in which there is sentiment enough to carry a woman suffrage amendment, but it is individual not organized sentiment, and is, therefore, uneffective!"

Mrs. Chapman Catt had stepped on some very tender toes. But Miss Susan had the good will to smile when she rose and said: "There never was a young woman who did not feel that if she had had the management of the work from the beginning the cause would have been carried long ago. I felt just so when I was young."

Miss Susan, at the same session, made another memorable comment: "One reason why politicians hesitate to grant suffrage to woman is because she is an unknown quantity. There are two great unknown forces today, electricity and woman, but men can reckon much better on electricity than they can on woman."

What probably shocked the "old-timers" in the movement was Mrs. Catt's emphasis on fund-raising. According to what the leaders considered to be its needs, the National American was reasonably prosperous. It annually reported between $9,000 and $14,000 in its national treasury. This was more than ample to pay the expenses of the annual convention which entertained somewhat lavishly. It provided for some publication, and paid the expenses of some of the less well-heeled representatives who were sent into states where woman suffrage amendments were before state legislatures.

But Carrie Catt was not talking about financing the annual convention or a few expense accounts. She was talking about money in politics, the money necessary to get a suffrage amendment through the Kansas legislature. She didn't mean using it as the liquor lobby would apply it. She just meant making sure that everyone was informed;

that there was money for newspaper advertising, campaign literature, and bands if necessary. And the next year, Mrs. Catt opened permanent headquarters in Philadelphia with a paid executive secretary. Now the files of the National American came out of Susan Anthony's parlor.

With Rachel Foster Avery in the Philadelphia office, Mrs. Catt focused her attack on the Iowa legislature, which was about to consider a woman suffrage movement. Ten thousand letters were mailed out from national head-quarters into the Hawkeye State. While Rachel Avery was pouring out this flood of printed matter, Mrs. Catt was operating out of Des Moines, supervising the organization of a thousand meetings. When, on a close roll call, the suffrage amendment was defeated, she didn't stop to grieve. She was convinced that the small margin of opposition would collapse before the next session of the legislature, so she just packed her bags and took off for Illinois and the South.

Now Mrs. Catt showed a boldness which was to be characteristic of her later career as the supreme pilot of woman suffrage. Instead of pleading with governors and congressmen, she went after powerful organizations which influenced votes. Her first great victory was the National Grange, and she didn't have to work very hard to win it.

The Patrons of Husbandry, better known as the Grange, had its birth in the severe economic depression of 1873. The farmers of the Midwest found themselves in an economic vise. The unethical financiers of New York were depressing the price of wheat and, at the same time, driving up freight rates to a point where the farmers couldn't afford to ship their produce.

Out of this impossible situation came the Patrons of Husbandry, a partly social, partly fraternal, and very much a political organization. Soon, because the Patrons also enlisted "patronesses," the organization came to be known as the Grange. It sponsored farm cooperatives, mass purchases of farm equipment, a forerunner of modern credit unions, mass sales, chicken-pie suppers, and farm legislation. By 1898, the Grange in the Midwest had become as politically powerful as the Grand Army of the Republic had been in the 1870's.

From its founding, the Grange had admitted women on an equal basis with men. They held offices in the lodges, spoke freely at policy meetings, voted for officers, and cooked the chicken pies. Mrs. Catt saw the great potentialities of Grange support. Since it already was a strong political force, why shouldn't the Grangers be eager to double their voting strength by enfranchising their women? Mrs. Catt went to the national leaders and asked them for an endorsement of a woman suffrage amendment to the Federal Constitution. The answer was "Yes," and she was probably told that they had been waiting to be asked for twenty years.

Now the time for the National American convention of 1900 was approaching, the dawn of a new century, and Susan Anthony called Carrie Catt to her home. Miss Susan announced that she would retire. She said that at eighty her body and mind were as sound as ever, and that she intended to work as hard as ever for the cause. But she had watched the bold tactics of Mrs. Catt and was convinced that they were essential to the final push which would bring a relatively quick victory.

Mrs. Catt didn't say that she wouldn't like to be president of the National American. She was never a hypocrite, but with her roughshod tactics at previous national conventions, she doubted that she could be elected. Miss Anthony assured her that she would pass the word around, and she was sure that the Association would accept her choice.

The convention of the National American Woman Suffrage Association opened on February 8, 1900, in Washington, with Susan Anthony in the chair. An observer wrote: "As she rose to open the convention, clad as usual in soft black satin, with duchess lace in the neck and sleeves and the lovely red crepe shawl falling gracefully from her shoulders, there was many a moist eye and tightened throat at the thought that this was the last time." Yes, Miss Susan had passed the word around.

Mrs. Chapman Catt was asked for her report, which included visiting twenty states during the past year and attending an equal number of state suffrage conventions. Her press committee reported that 31,800 press releases had been sent out from the Philadelphia headquarters.

Then Susan Anthony spoke: "I wish you could realize with what joy and relief I retire from the presidency. I want to say this to you while I am still alive — and I am good yet for another decade — don't be afraid. As long as my name stands at the head [she was to become honorary president], I am Yankee enough to feel that I must watch every potato which goes into the dinner pot. Four years ago I fixed my date for retirement. I am now going to let go of the machinery but not of the spiritual part."

Mrs. Catt had made a valid appraisal when she predicted that she would have opposition for the presidency of the National American. As the balloting approached, it appeared that a substantial part of the delegates were rallying behind Mrs. Lillie Devereux Blake of New York who was an avowed candidate. But Miss Susan had passed the word, and effectively. After her nomination had been seconded, Mrs. Blake took the stage and withdrew her candidacy. There was only one ballot: Mrs. Chapman Catt — 254; eleven for Miss Anthony, and ten for Mrs. Blake.

10 *The Day They Hissed the President*

At the outlet of New Hampshire's Lake Winnipesaukee, there stands on the shore a granite canopy, and under the canopy is a boulder marking the spot where, in 1692, a band of explorers sent by Governor Endicott of Massachusetts discovered the source of the Merrimack River. Atop the granite canopy is a bronze statue of a seminude Indian maiden. The maiden has never looked as though she were interested in politics, but on a July morning in 1914, when the mail steamer *Uncle Sam* steamed up the channel, a cheer went up from the passengers, for the Indian maiden's bare bosom was now covered with a bright yellow sash, and lettered upon it in blue was the legend VOTES FOR WOMEN.

Now it is most certain that Carrie Chapman Catt had nothing to do with using Endicott Rock for a publicity stunt, but whoever put the sash on the maiden was following a Catt-like technique. Now, with Lucy Stone gone and Miss Susan retired, Mrs. Catt was the "boss" of a perfectly coordinated organization. Strategy could be more flexible, shifting quickly and striking hard at the weak spots in the male political armor. Men who had respected but perhaps disagreed with Susan Anthony, either despised Carrie Catt or rallied to her cause with enthusiasm.

A term that was first applied by the press, and then adopted by Mrs. Catt, appropriately described the public image of the suffrage movement of that period. The era of Hearst-Pulitzer "yellow journalism" saw a great change in the Anglo-American vocabulary. To crowd the most news possible into the least newspaper space, contractions of words began to appear and were adopted by the public. The new self-service restaurant became the "cafeteria." Horse racing became "turfdom," and the 1904 Stevens-Duryea roadster burned "gas." And so the woman suffragists, after the turn of the century, became "suffragettes." It is difficult to estimate how much this newspaper contraction did for Mrs. Catt's regime.

Just using the diminutive suffix "ette" created the image of a young, active, sophisticated woman, in place of the woman suffragist — a somber, serious, dedicated social reformer. Suffragette just didn't go with the image of Lucretia Mott or Elizabeth Stanton. The suffragette was a Gibson Girl, a graduate of Vassar, Bryn Mawr, Smith, or Mount Holyoke. The suffragette had no interest in the temperance movement. She played tennis, and might even smoke a cigarette if no one was looking.

But Carrie Catt had another type of suffragette who didn't play tennis or drive a two-cylinder Winton. She was the laboring woman whose working conditions had improved but little since the Civil War. She was the Jewish immigrant working in New York's garment district under sweatshop conditions. And she was a member of the International Ladies Garment Workers' Union, which would soon endorse woman suffrage.

One of the most radical changes Mrs. Chapman Catt effected in the National American was in the character of the national conventions. For fifty years, the conventions had spelled little but talk-talk-talk. After 1900, there was still a day of speeches, but now the rest of the convention was devoted to workshops, a new word applied to breaking up into discussion groups. Groups of delegates devoted workshops to such subjects as "How to get the maximum press coverage and how to write news releases," "How to conduct a campaign," and "How to work with Labor."

The latter workshop topic reveals another very potent talent in the personality of Mrs. Catt: knowing how to work with and use other organizations. From Lucretia Mott to Mrs. Catt's administration, the cooperation between the suffrage movement and other reform organizations had been ineffectual if not damaging to the suffrage cause. First there had been Abolition, with the Abolitionists deserting the women after the passage of the Fourteenth Amendment. Then came Temperance, which drained off much needed energy and workers from the suffrage cause.

Now, when Mrs. Catt cooperated with another organization, she expected something concrete in return. She did not use the woman power of the National American unless the suffrage movement would benefit from the association. Her first "deal" was with Labor, previously ignored by the suffragists.

In the early 1900's there was much agitation for child-labor laws. Many industrialists opposed such legislation, because children under sixteen years of age could be hired to work under vile, health-destroying conditions for half the price of adult labor. Foremost in support of child-labor legislation was organized labor. Not only was its attitude humane, it was also defensive. Workers were walking the streets because children were taking their jobs. Mrs. Catt saw her chance. Going to Samuel Gompers, president of the American Federation of Labor, she offered the full support and facilities of the National American, provided the now powerful A.F.L. would support woman suffrage. Gompers agreed.

She set up other alliances with the National Council of Jewish Women, and for the first time invited prominent rabbis to speak at the conventions; The National Council of Charities and Corrections; The New York Consumers' League; The Federation of Women's Clubs; The National Forestry Association; and the Y.W.C.A. In return for their support, she invited the organizations to send their speakers to her national conventions.

Another brilliant talent of Mrs. Catt was in getting the most "publicity mileage" out of her conventions. At the same time she recognized, as had none of her predecessors, that the most fertile soil for woman suffrage was in the West. It had begun there. In the summer of 1905, Portland, Oregon, was to hold its great Lewis and Clark Exposition, the first world's fair in the West. Portland businessmen, eager for convention dollars, offered Mrs. Catt a tidy sum if she would bring the National American to Portland during the Exposition, and they promised to set aside one day as Ladies' Day. Mrs. Catt agreed.

Now, she saw an opportunity for a spectacular transcontinental caravan with all the trappings of a presidential campaign. To her staff she added a "railroad secretary," who made arrangements for a special train from Washington to Portland. The back platform of Mrs. Catt's private car at the rear of the train was decked with yellow and blue bunting, and there was a baggage car full of suffrage literature.

The Suffragette Special arrived in Chicago on June 23, where it picked up three more carloads of delegates from New York and New England. In the Windy City a huge reception was given for Susan Anthony, who was riding with Mrs. Catt. The rest of the trip to Portland was typical of a first-rate "whistle-stop" campaign. Mrs. Catt's advance agents had crowds out at every stop where Mrs. Catt and Miss Anthony made rear-platform appearances, or speeches if the crowds were large enough. There was a two-hour stop at Cheyenne, Wyoming, to honor the birthplace of woman suffrage. As the train neared Portland, a Negro Pullman porter remarked to Mrs. Catt's railroad clerk, "I ain't never traveled with such a bunch of women before — they don't fuss with me and they don't scrap with each other!"

The Suffragette Special had attracted the attention of the nation's press, and now Mrs. Chapman Catt would keep it focused on the convention which opened on June 28. In spite of the fact that the Exposition was in full swing, the Associated Press kept a staff man at Mrs. Catt's headquarters from the day she arrived.

Then came Ladies' Day at the Exposition, and a band playing "Ault Lang Syne" escorted Susan Anthony to the main pavilion. There, Mrs. Catt made another one of her "alliances" with Hon. W. S. U'Ren, known as the "father of Initiative and Referendum." Under I & R, the citizens of a state may, with a petition bearing the requisite number of signatures, force a bill, on which the legislature has refused to act, to be submitted to the electorate. Mrs. Catt threw her support to I & R not only in return for Mr. U'Ren's endorsement of woman suffrage, but because I & R could force action on woman suffrage amendments where they had lost by small margins in the state legislatures.

As the Suffragette Special chugged its way back across

the Western plains, and the AP staff man was taking down Mrs. Catt's reactions to the Portland Exposition, she could sum it up: "This was the highwater mark of fifty-five years. More effective columns of newspaper space have been devoted to the movement than ever before. Never again will suffrage cease to be front-page copy."

But Mrs. Chapman Catt's headlines were now arousing uneasiness among some of the nation's political and spiritual leaders: Cardinal Gibbons of Baltimore, former President Grover Cleveland, and President Theodore Roosevelt. Grover Cleveland had written in the April issue of the *Ladies Home Journal* advising women not to join clubs except those with "purposes of charity, religious enterprise, or intellectual improvement. . . . Her best and safest club is her home." In the October issue he followed with: "Sensible and responsible women do not want to vote. The relative positions to be assumed by man and woman in the working out of our civilization were assigned long ago by a higher intelligence than ours."

When asked by an interviewer what he thought of women joining woman suffrage organizations, Cardinal Gibbons replied, "A Society like the Daughters of the American Revolution I heartily approve of . . . but other clubs of all kinds I heartily disapprove of."

From the White House came the pronouncement: "The President of the United States does not absent himself from the country during the term of his Presidency, it is his domain. So it will be with woman; she is the queen of her empire and that empire is the home." Just six years later, "Teddy" Roosevelt changed the boundaries of the queen's empire when he was running for President on the Progressive ticket and desperately needed women's votes in states where they had the franchise.

But in spite of Cardinal Gibbons's opposition, one of the encouraging tendencies of the period was the increasing support of equal rights by the clergy of all faiths. Some were even questioning the validity of St. Paul's statements on women. Soon after President Roosevelt's "queen's empire" statement, a New York clergyman wrote, "Some pulpits may insist that Paul was infallible, but I prefer to believe that he was human and liable to err. I have come to think that Paul was never equalled in his advice to wife, mother, and maiden aunt except by the present occupant of the White House, Theodore Roosevelt."

Another bright star on the suffrage horizon was the increasing involvement of college students, both female and male. This disturbed some of the "old guard" of the suffrage movement. This wasn't in the Stone-Stanton tradition. These girls from Vassar rode their bicycles (very unladylike) with yellow and blue ribbons woven into the spokes of their wheels and with VOTES FOR WOMEN placards tied to their handlebars. These aggressive girls had organized branches of the National College Women's Suffrage League in fifteen states, and College Night had become a feature of Mrs. Catt's national conventions.

These young women of the National College Women's Suffrage League brought a new title to this segment of the movement. They came to be known as the "the Militants." The motto of the Militants was "INTO THE STREETS!" and they launched a campaign of nonviolent protest before Dr. Martin Luther King was born into this world.

Inspired by news reports of a march in London by 10,000 women to impress Parliament that they meant business, the Militants took to the streets at Northampton, Massachusetts. The Smith College Marching Militants began precision drilling. Some of the marching units had male auxiliaries of college boys, and this disturbed the oldsters of the National American. Would college boys be appearing at the national conventions with stinking pipes, cigarettes, and beer? What would the temperance leaders say?

Marching required music, and not since the Hutchinson family had ridden on a float in Kansas had music played so much of a part in the suffrage movement beyond a few of Miss Susan's favorite hymns at the national conventions. Now a whole repertoire of suffragette music was demanded, and the songs poured forth. Here are a few:

Uncle Sam's Wedding
(Tune: "Yankee Doodle")

Of all the songs that have been sung
Within the States and Nation,
There's none that comes so near the heart
As Uncle Sam's relation.
When Uncle Sam set up his house,
He welcomed ev'ry brother,
But in his haste of his new life,
He quite forgot his mother.
Now his house is up in arms,
A keeper he must find him
To sweep and dust and set to rights
The tangles all about him.
Uncle Sam is long in years,
And he is growing wiser;
He now can see 'twas a mistake
To have no Miss-advisor.

And another —

Giving the Ballot to the Mothers
(Tune: "Marching Through Georgia")
Bring the good old bugle, boys!
We'll sing another song.

Sing it with a spirit that will
Start the cause along.
Sing it as we ought to sing it,
Cheerily and strong;
Giving the ballots to the mothers!"
Bring the dear old banner, boys,
And fling it to the wind;
Mother, wife and daughter
Let it shelter and defend.
"Equal Rights our motto is,
We're loyal to the end —
Giving the ballots to the mothers!"

And still another —

The Taxation Tyranny
(Tune: "Columbia the Gem of the Ocean")
To tax one who's not represented
Is tyranny — tell if you can
Why women should not have the ballot?
She's taxed just the same as the man.
King George, you remember, denied us
The ballot, but sent us the tea.
And we, without asking a question,
Just tumbled it into the sea.

Chorus:
Then to justice let's ever be true,
To each citizen render his due.
Equal rights and protection forever
To all 'neath the Red, White and Blue!

That one man shall not rule another,
Unless by the other's consent,
Is the principle deep underlying
The framework of this government.
So, as woman is punished for breaking

> The laws which she cannot gainsay,
> Let us give her a voice in the making,
> Or ask her no more to obey.

Shades of gentle, quiet Lucy Stone and the peaceful Quaker, Lucretia Mott! Society matrons shuddered when they saw young women marching in the streets, well drilled and shouting their suffragette songs. But many of their daughters were out there in the ranks. Bankers, driving to their offices in the morning, snorted when they saw VOTES FOR WOMEN crudely painted in large letters on a board fence, but their daughters had done the painting. There were catcalls from the curbs, rotten eggs, and overripe tomatoes greeted the marchers, but they marched and sang just the same — and Mrs. Chapman Catt cheered.

In Great Britain, the Militants were outdoing their American sisters. Speaking to the National American convention, British Mrs. Snowden reported: "The militancy thus far has *only* consisted of heckling speakers, getting into the gallery of the House of Commons and yelling 'Votes for Women,' and breaking windows in government buildings, a time-honored English custom of showing disapproval."

Of Mrs. Snowden's report, Mrs. Catt said, "The path has been blazed for us and they have shown us the way. It is the hour for us to rally. We have enlisted for the war." Breaking windows and all, we presume.

At the national convention of the National American Woman Suffrage Association of 1910, held in Washington, for the first time, the presiding officer announced: "Ladies and gentlemen, *the President of the United States!*"

President William Howard Taft mounted the platform. He had been invited to address the convention with the understanding that his appearance would not be regarded as committing him to the advocacy of woman suffrage. Taft accepted over the loud protest of Mrs. Elihu Root, wife of President Roosevelt's Secretary of State, and an officer of the Anti-Suffrage Association. Naturally, there was great curiosity over what the President would say. The convention was not long in finding out where he stood, and he was the first President to be hissed by a convention of women.

The President began by saying that as a high school junior he had made a speech before an assembly advocating woman suffrage. He explained: "I had read Mill's *Subjection of Women;* my father was a suffragist and so was I. But in actual political experience which I have had, I have modified my views somewhat."

Then Taft clarified his attitude: "I call your attention to two qualifications — that in a popular representative government, every class intelligent enough to vote should do so: but I call to your attention two qualifications in that statement. . . . The theory that Hottentots or any other uneducated, altogether unintelligent class is fitted for self-government at once . . . is a theory I wholly dissent from — but this theory is not fitted here [he hastened to get that one in, the women were ready to walk out]. The other qualification to which I call your attention is that the class should care as a whole enough to look after its interests, to take part *as a whole* in the exercise of political power if it is conferred. It seems to me that the danger is, if the power is conferred, that it may be exercised by that part of the class least desirable as political constituents, and be neglected by many of those who are intelligent and patriotic."

Here the hissing started, and it was loud and clear. The shock of a President of the United States being hissed probably would have set Taft back on his haunches had they not been supporting the largest presidential belly in American history. (At one time he became helplessly wedged into the White House bathtub.) Of course, the officers of the convention were supremely embarrassed, but Taft had certainly "asked for it."

In the first place, he shouldn't have mentioned Hottentots if he had to explain immediately that he wasn't classifying Susan Anthony with an African aborigine. Furthermore, what he meant to say was not what he implied. What the President meant to say, as unpopular as it would have been if understood, was that intelligent women wouldn't vote, and that the political bosses would round up women of questionable character to stuff ballot boxes. That was bad enough, because it implied that if Carrie Chapman Catt and the Smith College Marching Militants were really intelligent, they wouldn't be interested in voting. But worse, on the surface Taft's statement could be taken as implying that Mrs. Elihu Root was an intelligent, decent patriotic lady who didn't want to vote. But where did that put Mrs. Chapman Catt? Taft's greatest blunder was in overlooking the fact that there were delegates present from four states where women had the full franchise and where they had been voting for years. Observers at the convention said that most of the hissing came from the delegates of Wyoming, Colorado, Utah, and Idaho. Taft was to regret his words on the morning after the 1912 presidential election.

The convention immediately passed a resolution apologizing to the President for the unfortunate incident, but it concluded with the warning: "The women of America intend to make themselves directly felt in the government of which he [Taft] is the honored head, and at no distant date."

The annual petition to Congress that year was as different from past procedure as anything could be. Mrs. Catt didn't ride to the Capitol with her aides in a carriage. Instead, there was a well-organized parade of fifty automobiles which chugged and sputtered their way down Pennsylvania Avenue. They were decorated with American flags and yellow and blue suffragette emblems. There was a float with petitions to congressmen piled head high. There was no disrespect from the sidewalks, and a new kind of respect when the motorcade reached the Capitol. During the presentation of the petitions in both Houses, *while they were in session,* "Fighting Bob" La Follette of Wisconsin rose and said, "I hope the time will come when this great body of intelligent people will not find it necessary to petition for that which ought to be accorded as a right in a country of equal opportunity."

But the most spectacular proof of the onrushing suffrage victory was the report read at the convention of forty powerful labor organizations which had endorsed the crusade during the past year, including the venerable International Typographical Union.

The years 1911 and 1912 are perhaps the most dramatic in the history of woman suffrage. So many things happened so fast. Even the final victorious roll call is an anticlimax, because by 1919, the strength of the Suffragettes was invincible, and the vote was a push-over.

At the 1910 election in the state of Washington, the suffrage amendment had carried by a vote of three to one. When the 1911 National American convention met in Louisville, its chairman could report that the legislatures of Kansas, Oregon, Wisconsin, and Nevada had voted to submit suffrage amendments to the voters, and the chances of victory appeared excellent. Added to the impetus of the National College Women's Suffrage League, with its singing, militant marchers, was the new National Men's Suffrage League with a membership of some 20,000. Now, "Giving the Ballot to the Mothers" could be sung in four-part harmony.

For a time in 1910, Mrs. Catt was forced by fatigue to take a rest, while the militants carried on in the streets. But in 1911, she completed a round-the-world tour to campaign for the cause and also to feel its pulse abroad. At the 1911 convention, Mrs. Catt, just returned, reported a tidal wave of sentiment for equal suffrage from Finland to Japan. The cheering delegates to this convention were further inspired by the appearance of Mrs. Emmeline Pankhurst, the British Susan Anthony. But unlike stately Susan, Mrs. Pankhurst had been a militant since her conversion to the suffrage movement. She had led the women when they threw rocks through the windows of Parliament, and she was still throwing them.

Mrs. Pankhurst told the delegates that after the women of Britain had unsuccessfully tried every constitutional means of winning the vote, they had *revolted* in the fullest sense of the word. They had marched, blocked traffic, thrown rocks, chained themselves to the gates of Parliament, and staged sit-ins. In return they had been mobbed, beaten by the police, thrown in jail by the dozen, and further brutalized. But the demonstrations were continuing unhalted.

But joyous 1911 was only a prelude to 1912. The log jamb was breaking and there was every sign that it would soon collapse entirely. Nineteen twelve would be the year, not for victory perhaps, but for the women to make the greatest show of all. The stage was set for them to make themselves felt in a presidential election. Now the national party conventions would be on the spot. Would President Taft perhaps want to eat the words he had spoken to the ladies in 1910? With the electoral votes, which might be controlled by women in a close election, now tripled, the national party conventions could not avoid debates on suffrage planks in the two platforms. The delegates from at least eight states would insist on that. One of the most likely candidates for the Democratic presidential nomination, Governor Woodrow Wilson of New Jersey, was believed to be an "Anti." He would be asked to make his position very clear.

There were rumblings and grumblings which gave an indication that 1912 would be a great year for the suffragettes. They came from within the Republican Party, from a group of Midwesterners and Westerners, later to be dubbed by New Hampshire's Senator George H. Moses as "the Sons of the Wild Jackass." Their leaders were Senator "Fighting Bob" La Follette of Wisconsin, Senator William E. Borah of Idaho, and Governor Hiram Johnson of California. They were bitterly opposed to Taft's conservative policies, and they all favored equal suffrage.

There was another, not currently an office holder, and certainly not a feminist, who had presidential ambitions on a liberal platform — Theodore Roosevelt. As President, filling out McKinley's term, he had been unpopular with conservative Republicans, and he was passed over by the 1906 convention. Although he was supposed to have retired, he continued to make headlines.

As the 1912 calendars were being mailed out from patent medicine firms and Pears Soap, it appeared that one million women could vote that year. Taft and the conservatives in both parties should have marked that down. On February 27, Roosevelt announced that he would run for the Republican nomination. In the Democratic Party it appeared that the contest would be between Governor Wilson of New Jersey and the perennial candidate, William Jennings Bryan. To the one million women voters, three million pieces of mail had gone out from the National American Association. It was as fully organized nationally as both major political parties.

One of the closest friends of the Roosevelt family had been Julia Ward Howe of Boston, the suffrage leader in

Massachusetts and an important influence nationally. Mrs. Howe died in 1910, and her daughter, Maud Howe Elliott, carried on both her mother's work and her friendship with Theodore Roosevelt. By the latter part of 1911, Mrs. Elliott was deeply involved in the Roosevelt-for-President movement, although at the time she did not know his position on equal rights. On February 1, 1912, Mrs. Elliott received a letter from the former President, asking her to visit him. At his office he showed her an article he had just written for *Outlook* magazine, in which he paid tribute to Julia Ward Howe and everything she stood for, including woman suffrage. Then he said, "You know that neither my mother nor my wife is in favor of suffrage. I believe that your mother more than anyone else converted me to it." Two weeks later he publicly announced his candidacy, but those two weeks gave Maud Howe Elliott time to shower the state suffrage associations with telegrams stating that "Teddy is for Us."

Mrs. Elliott's next venture was to organize a huge equal rights parade in New York City which marched on May 4. It was led by girls on horseback. The feature of the parade was a large banner carrying a large portrait of Julia Ward Howe with the legend: "He hath sounded forth the trumpet that shall never call retreat," and there could be no doubt in anyone's mind who had sounded forth the trumpet.

On June 11, 1912, Roosevelt was defeated by Taft for the Republican nomination, and he immediately announced that he would organize a third party, the Progressive. The Republicans, after shunning Roosevelt, had refused to place an equal rights plank in their platform. The Democrats nominated Woodrow Wilson and ignored the women.

Now, the National American Association faced a serious dilemma. An unwritten law prohibited its officers from taking part in partisan politics. But here were three presidential candidates: Taft, Republican, who believed that only ignorant women would vote if given the franchise; Woodrow Wilson, Democrat, born a Virginian and with the Southern male prejudice against women in politics; and Teddy Roosevelt, Progressive, who had come out openly for woman suffrage, and the Progressive Party had adopted a woman suffrage plank. The unwritten law of the Association reflected the pessimism of the early leaders: that they would never have the opportunity to make a choice between a presidential candidate who favored equal rights and one who didn't.

There is no indication that any of the top leaders in the national organization took any active part in the campaign of 1912, but the prohibition had little effect on the state suffrage association officers. By August, Mrs. Elliott was women's Roosevelt-for-President state chairman in Rhode Island. She also worked with the New England Roosevelt headquarters in Boston. Everywhere she went, bands played the "Battle Hymn," which meant "Roosevelt and Suffrage." On election night, Mrs. Elliott wrote in her diary, "Remained until midnight at headquarters for the election returns that were confusing enough, but prepared us for the news of Wilson's election in the morning."

The forty-fourth annual convention of the National American Suffrage Association met in Philadelphia two weeks after the presidential election, and the atmosphere was both jubilant and concerned. The women voters had helped to topple the most powerful candidate in the election, William Howard Taft, and he publicly attributed his defeat to "the emotional votes of women." Oregon, Kansas, Arizona, and California had amended their state constitutions, and in Michigan the vote had been so close that a recount was still going on.

The importance of the Association as a source of national and international news is highlighted by the report of the organization's press secretary, Miss Caroline Reilly. She said, "The winning of California wrought a complete change in the work of our national press bureau. Before that victory our time was employed in furnishing suffragette arguments, replying to adverse editorials and writing syndicate articles. Now this department has resolved itself into a bureau of information. We now have twenty syndicates on our list and are no longer required to write the articles ourselves but simply supply the information which their own writers work up. Last week, a representative of a European syndicate came and said that he had been sent to America for the sole purpose of reporting the woman movement in the United States, the subject being regarded a vital one by the press of Europe."

But in the midst of jubilation, a bitter controversy broke out. It was over the extensive partisan campaigning which many of the state leaders had carried on for Roosevelt and the Progressive ticket. A resolution preventing members of the Association from politicking was finally defeated, ten to one, but another resolution was adopted barring national officers from partisan activity.

The thinking and planning of the National American just couldn't keep up with its success. They were right in maintaining that the national organization, fighting for an amendment to the Federal Constitution, could not afford to offend either major political party. But what they couldn't seem to comprehend were the members who were already voters. The women of Wyoming had been Democrats or Republicans since 1869. Now, thousands of California women belonged to and campaigned for one of the two parties. Even a leader as astute as Carrie Chapman Catt, couldn't seem to face the political fact that with every additional state granting woman suffrage, just so many more of her membership were immediately up to their necks in politics. They were proving that the woman vote was a good influence, but the women voted Democratic or Republican.

By 1913 the log jamb loosened further. Mighty Illinois, with its potent electoral vote, granted suffrage, followed by the Alaska Territory. Legislation was pending in Nevada, Montana, North Dakota, and South Dakota. Initiative petitions were being circulated in Ohio, Nebraska and Missouri.

On the day before President-elect Wilson's inauguration, the women stole a march. Washington was jammed with visitors. Pennsylvania Avenue was decorated for the march to the Capitol, and everyone was in a holiday mood. Suddenly bands were heard on "the Avenue." Men came out of the saloons and hotels to see what was going on, expecting that the Democrats were having a pre-inaugural celebration; but no, the marchers were all women. Mrs. Alice Roosevelt Longworth, daughter of Theodore Roosevelt and husband of the Speaker of the House, was there. She later wrote, "The day before the Inauguration the woman suffragists had a huge parade, Inez Mulholland riding at the head, which I ended by seeing from a lunch wagon."

This demonstration had been secretly organized by Mrs. Catt's Association. The participants, 8,000, instead of coming by train, where their numbers and special cars would have given warning that something was in the air, came by automobiles: Reos, Saxons, Hupmobiles, and Winton Sixes.

"Princess Alice" Roosevelt (Mrs. Nicholas Longworth) whose famous father tacitly endorsed the suffragists cause.

Inez Mulholland (left) is dressed in symbolic white. With her is Mrs. Richard Coke Burleson, grand marshall of the suffragists' parade in Washington.

The public reaction to this great demonstration was adverse, frightening, and a portent of things to come. The Democrats were furious, for the parade had temporarily removed the spotlight from their victory and would steal space in the Inauguration Day newspapers. The few Republicans remaining in Washington glared at the marching ladies, reminded that they had helped to send their party down to defeat. As Woodrow Wilson looked down on the parade from his window in Willard's Hotel, he must have pondered that, if he intended running for a second term, he might have to revise his thinking on women in politics.

The Association waited hopefully for some mention of equal rights in the President's first message to Congress, whether for or against, but he failed to mention it. Ruth Hanna McCormick, as astute a politician, as her father, Mark Hanna, remarked, "Since President Wilson omitted all mention of woman suffrage in his message yesterday, I move that we wait on him in order to lay before him the importance of the question, that he may take it up in future speeches." There were several million dollars behind that suggestion.

A delegation called on Wilson, presented their case and quoted from his book, *The New Freedom*. One of the delegates reported: "He was very courteous, but his attitude was one of amused curiosity." Soon the amusement would disappear, and his attitude would change radically during the next seven years.

Now Mrs. Catt's organization began to demonstrate in earnest, only to find out that it had a tiger by the tail. Previously, her cry "Into the streets" had been confined to the militants. But the success of the March 3 parade in Washington demanded a series of follow-ups. On April 7,

Ruth Hanna McCormick, daughter of shrewd Mark Hanna, tried to get Woodrow Wilson behind the woman's suffrage movement.

a large motorcade of women paraded through Washington to the Senate. In July there was a series of "pilgrimages" from all over the country to present petitions bearing 200,000 signatures to the Senate. Three more delegations called on the President, one composed of seventy-three women from Wilson's New Jersey. During the vacation season, a paid organizer arranged demonstrations in the resort areas: New Jersey, Long Island, and Rhode Island. Suffrage had cracked the society set. A number of congressmen were recruited into the Men's Suffrage League. Suffrage plays, written by professional dramatists, were being given in cities throughout the East, and a suffrage tableau was staged on the steps of the U.S. Treasury. Parades as large as the pre-inaugural demonstrations were held in Boston, New York, and Baltimore.

Congress was beginning to feel the pressure, and the Senate Committee on Woman Suffrage was now in the hands of those who favored the franchise for women. However, they could not agree on how it should be accomplished, some favoring a law to permit all women to vote for President, some for permitting women to vote for President and members of Congress, but not for state elective officials unless the states passed necessary legislation.

The great single barrier to a suffrage amendment to the Constitution was the House of Representatives, where the Democrats were solidly in control and where most important committees had conservative Southerners as chairmen. While the Senate ·had had its Committee on Woman Suffrage since 1883, in the House all woman suffrage legislation was referred to the Judiciary Committee where it was always buried. It was buried by a coalition of conservative Democrats and Republicans and the big city

machines. All three factions opposed woman suffrage because they liked things as they were, and they were afraid
that women with votes would upset the applecart. Obviously, there would have to be some "arm-twisting" on
the part of the National American Association, and now it
had the strength to do it.

On June 26, 1914, the Austrian Archduke Francis Ferdinand was assassinated in Sarajevo, Serbia, now a part of Yugoslavia. Austria declared war on Serbia, and soon this little Balkan bonfire roared into the holocaust of World War I. President Wilson was pleading for peace and insisting on the neutrality of the United States. The American mothers were praying for peace, but the National American Association was preparing for war on the home front, and it had plenty of ammunition.

That year, Nevada adopted woman suffrage with a landslide vote. Secretary of State William Jennings Bryan had endorsed equal rights. For the first time, the proposed woman suffrage amendment was reported out of the House Judiciary Committee, and the Democratic leadership was in panic. Fearing that enough western Democrats and northern Republicans might supply the necessary two-thirds vote to pass the amendment, and realizing that it would receive more generous treatment in the Senate, the House Democrats caucused and voted 123 to 55 not to call up the amendment.

Now Mrs. Catt not only had a headquarters in Washington, she also operated a well-organized congressional lobby. Individual congressmen were no longer petitioned; they were pressured. Every roll call pertaining to women was scanned by Mrs. Catt's lobbyists, and the vote of every congressman was recorded and sent back to the woman suffrage association in his state. The desperation of the anti-suffragists is typified by a phone call received by Elinor Brynes, Mrs. Catt's ace publicity director. She reported: "A few months ago a writer for one of the 'Anti' newspapers in New York called me and said, 'I have been asked to write an editorial on the menace of woman suffrage. Can you help me?' 'Yes,' I replied; 'I can prove that the majority of presidential electors in 1916 may represent equal suffrage states, and that in all probability every political party will have to endorse woman suffrage before that time. What could be worse than that?' "

But in this time of great strength, when $50,000 could be pledged in a single session of the women's national conventions, and while the number of pro-suffrage congressmen was steadily growing, a rift developed in the National American Suffrage Association which did not impede the march of equal rights, but caused some strained congressional relations.

The Militant Suffragettes, those who followed the tactics of British Mrs. Pankhurst in marching, rock throwing, pummeling policemen, and getting jailed, were restless under the leadership of Mrs. Catt. They seceded from the National American Association and formed the Congressional Union. Probably Mrs. Catt was not sorry to be relieved of the blame for broken windows, but now the new Congressional Union turned political. It blamed the entire Democratic Party for the delaying tactics of the House

Judiciary Committee and for President Wilson's states' rights position. It campaigned against the Democratic Party in every state where it had an organization. Worse than that, to the man of 1914, they picketed the White House. This does not seem shocking today when picketing the White House is a common occurrence, but in 1914 this was considered a gross indignity against the Presidency.

The unjust tactics of the Congressional Union were in attacking the Democratic Party everywhere, regardless of the stand taken on suffrage by the individual Democratic congressman, especially in the West. It opposed the re-election of a Democratic Senator from Colorado who was chairman of the Senate Committee on Woman Suffrage, and who had done more than any other senator to get a constitutional amendment on the floor of the Senate. It stiffened the resistance of some congressmen who were nearly ready to change their votes from "states' rights" to a federal amendment. And worst of all, congressmen who couldn't, or didn't want to understand the separation of the National American Association and the Congressional Union, blamed Mrs. Catt for meddling in Democratic politics.

In spite of this temporary discord, in the 1915 session of Congress the proposed Sixteenth Amendment reached the floor of the House of Representatives on December 22. It was defeated 204 to 174, the greatest "Aye" vote in suffrage history. Mrs. Catt now had only to win over thirty-one congressmen, and considerable pressure could be exerted before the 1916 election.

That fall of 1915, President Wilson, with an eye on the thirteen equal rights states with ninety-one electoral votes, went home to New Jersey to cast his ballot for a New Jersey suffrage amendment. He still believed that suffrage should be won state by state, but by now seven members

Suffragists wait on the east steps of the Capitol, to present President Woodrow Wilson with a petition from 4 million women, July 7, 1915.

of his Cabinet had openly endorsed an amendment to the Federal Constitution.

In preparation for the 1916 Presidential election, Mrs. Catt employed a crew of statisticians to survey state voting records over a period of twenty-five years in an attempt to predict the influence of the woman vote. She employed 120 press chairmen throughout the country and set up a substantial staff of feature writers in Washington to feed the Sunday newspaper supplements.

And now Carrie Chapman Catt won a most important supporter, in a way more important than the President himself — grizzled, dictatorial Champ Clark, Speaker of the House of Representatives. The power of the Speaker is enormous. He can throttle debate by refusing to recognize an opponent of the legislation he favors. His parliamentary rulings, whether just or unjust, are law. He can reward or punish congressmen with his control of committee appointments. The congressman who is consistently "right" in the eyes of the Speaker may sit on the Foreign Affairs Committee. The representative on the wrong side of the fence will get to the Committee on the Capitol Grounds. Champ Clark exercised all of these powers to the fullest, and now Carrie Catt had him on her side. She not only had the Speaker, but Mrs. Clark had offered to speak extensively for the cause.

Mrs. Catt planned carefully for the national party conventions and for the 1916 convention of her own organization. She made it clear that this year the politicians would be "on the asking end." The day preceding the opening of the Republican National Convention in Chicago she staged a mammoth suffrage parade financed by Mrs. Medill McCormick who was now generously opening her purse to the National American. A similar parade preceded the Democratic National Convention in St. Louis. The newspapers called the St. Louis parade "The River of Gold", because the thousands of women wore the yellow sashes with blue lettering, the official badge of equal rights. In New York City, 20,000 women marched up Fifth Avenue, sixteen abreast.

At both national party conventions, suffrage was fully debated both in committee and on the floor. Mrs. Catt's lobbyists were given unlimited time to present their arguments. For the first time, woman suffrage appeared in the platforms of both parties. Both parties endorsed it — in principle. Neither party pledged itself to support a constitutional amendment, and the Democratic plank was "softer" than the Republican version.

Woman's Suffrage parade on Fifth Avenue, 1915.

In the history of the equal rights movement, no presidential candidate had ever gone beyond his party's platform even though he believed in woman suffrage, as in the case of Garfield. But now Charles Evans Hughes, the Republican nominee, came out boldly on his own and pledged his support for a constitutional amendment. Now President Wilson, renominated for a second term, was on the spot, and Carrie Chapman Catt would be there too in a short time.

When the annual convention of the National American Association met in Atlantic City, the picture was far different from any which preceded it. The hotels and convention hall were crowded with political dignitaries. The wives of most of Wilson's Cabinet were there. Senators and congressmen abounded. Margaret Wilson, the President's daughter, was there wearing her yellow sash, and so was his other daughter, Mrs. William G. McAdoo, wife of the Secretary of the Treasury. Mrs. Champ Clark was on the platform.

Now came what could have been an embarrassing situation for Mrs. Catt. She had invited both presidential candidates to address the convention. Wilson had accepted, since he would be campaigning in New Jersey at the time. Hughes wrote that his itinerary would not make it possible for him to speak, but promised to send a state-ment which could be read to the delegates. Hughes's message arrived while Mrs. Catt was presiding at the evening session before the day President Wilson was scheduled to speak.

Mrs. Catt read the Republican candidate's message to

Mrs. Herbert S. Car-penter, grand marshal, sets a spirited pace for a New York State division parade.

the convention, and it was a wholehearted endorsement of universal suffrage by constitutional amendment. When she concluded, there was pandemonium in the convention hall, but Mrs. Catt wasn't cheering. Could she keep partisanship out of the National American if Wilson didn't come out positively for woman suffrage? And what would happen tomorrow when the President appeared? Would there be another "hissing incident" which had marred the only previous occasion when a President, Taft, had spoken to the delegates?

Tomorrow came, and with it the arrival of Woodrow Wilson. He had asked to be placed last on the program that he might sit through the session and listen to the other speakers. He heard speakers treat such subjects as "Why Women Need the Vote;" "The Call of the Working Woman," by Mrs. Raymond Robins, president of the National Women's Trades Union League; "Mothers in Politics;" "A Necessary Safeguard to Morals," by Dr. Katharine Davis, chief of the New York Parole Commission; "Working Children," by Dr. Owen R. Lovejoy, general Secretary of the National Child Labor Committee.

Now Mrs. Catt introduced the President. At first, he spoke in generalities of the complexity of modern life. He said: "As our life has unfurled and and accumulated, as the contacts of it have become hot, as the populations have assembled in the cities and the cool spaces of the country have been supplemented by feverish urban areas, the whole nature has been altered. They have ceased to be legal questions. They have more and more become social questions, questions with regard to the relations of human beings to one another."

Significantly commenting on the convention, he said: "I have felt as I sat here tonight the wholesome contagion of

About to advertise their cause in the subway at 72nd Street and Broadway, the suffragists display their placards.

A new "Liberty Bell" is cast in Troy, N.Y., April 1, 1915, to symbolize the movement's growing hope. At the ladle wheel is Mrs. Frank M. Roessing, president of the Pennsylvania association; at the extreme right is Mrs. Carrie Chapman Catt.

the occasion. Almost every time that I ever visited Atlantic City, I came to fight somebody [at political conventions]. I hardly know how to conduct myself when I have come not to fight anybody, *but with somebody.*"

The Democratic candidate concluded: "I have not come to ask you to be patient, because you have been, but I have come to congratulate you that there has been a force behind you that will beyond any peradventure be triumphant and for which you can afford a little while to wait."

Dr. Anna Shaw, honorary chairman of the convention, responded to the President: "We have waited long enough for the vote, we want it now." Then she smiled and continued: "And we want it to come in your administration."

What had Wilson really said? He had told them that their victory was inevitable; that he was fighting *with*, not against them; he had told them to wait awhile; and he had not used the words "constitutional amendment." The whole speech, tracing the sociology of America from the Revolution, could be summed up as saying, "I am in favor of woman suffrage somehow, sometime."

Woodrow Wilson went to bed on election night believing that he had probably lost the election. He awoke in the morning to find that he had "squeezed in" by a margin of twenty-three electoral votes, California's, and a popular plurality of only 591,385.

What the voting women contributed to the outcome cannot be assessed. One can be fairly certain that Hughes's statement to the Atlantic City convention helped, and Wilson's speech certainly did not help him. Most observers of the election agree that the greatest asset of the Democrats was the slogan "He Kept Us Out of War." That slogan would be meaningless within six months, and then the woman's rights movement would face its greatest test since 1861.

13 *Suffragettes in Uniform*

In 1917, those who were old enough to remember, or had read of the temporarily paralyzing effect of the Civil War on the woman's rights movement, and expected a repetition in World War I, were mightily imperceptive, or they greatly underestimated the genius of Mrs. Chapman Catt. Instead of losing her leaders to the war effort, she converted the National American Suffrage Association into a huge organization for war service. She made it into a great public display of woman's ability in wide fields of service. Instead of allowing the war to eclipse the movement, as had happened in 1861, she placed the National American in the public spotlight. It would be a safe estimate that World War I advanced the final passage of the Nineteenth Amendment by two years.

The 1917 National American Convention, held in Washington on December 12, forcefully demonstrated that annual conventions would be out of the question until after the war. Although unrelated to the war, the temperature was below zero. Because of the number of troop trains, some passenger trains arrived in Washington thirty-six hours late.

Delegates from the South went through two train wrecks. The hotel and convention facilities were so crowded with contractors, army officers, government workers, and draftees that the convention had to break down into small groups, many meeting in private homes. The delegates housed themselves as best they could, spilling out into neighboring Maryland and Virginia.

But in spite of the cold, the suffrage sun shone on the convention. The month before, New York had legalized woman suffrage. The House of Commons in London had voted seven to one for equal rights. France was sure to vote suffrage as soon as the invader was repelled. The Russian Revolution guaranteed the vote to its women, but didn't tell them how little they would have to vote for. On the second day of the convention, the House finally got around to vote itself a Committee on Woman Suffrage, thirty-four years after the Senate, and voting on the measure was Representative Jeanette Rankin of Montana, the first woman member of Congress.

The delegates canvassed the congressional delegations from their states and, for the most part, received friendly receptions, the exceptions being Virginia and South Carolina. President Wilson gave a reception for the delegation from Arkansas where woman suffrage had just been voted. Senator Warren G. Harding of Ohio appeared extremely cordial at the reception which he gave for the delegates from his state.

In one of the few opportunities which Mrs. Catt obtained to address all of the 600 delegates in one place, she pledged the entire National American to war work, she told the delegates that over 2,000 members of the organization were already overseas, working in hospitals, driving ambulances, and serving in the Red Cross. Then after a

Mrs. Jeanette Rankin, left, was the first woman to enter Congress. She is with Mrs. Bennett Champ Clark, right.

short address by Congresswoman Rankin, Mrs. Catt sent the delegates home to put their state organizations on a wartime footing and to staff every wartime service agency to the limit of their numbers.

Then on December 18, while the returning delegates were wrestling with wartime transportation, Congress passed a momentous piece of legislation which had more effect on the advancement of woman suffrage, the Eighteenth (Prohibition) Amendment. Most of the women supported Prohibition on moral and social grounds, but there were probably few who realized what it would do for them politically. They fell heirs to two great political advantages which would make their cause more invincible than ever.

First, Prohibition evaporated the political power of the liquor lobby in opposition to woman suffrage. There suddenly was no liquor industry excepting a small amount of distilling for medicinal purposes. The farmers who had sometimes sided with the liquor interests politically, because the distilleries bought their corn and barley, now could sell all they could grow to the government. The railroads, which had reaped revenue by transporting thousands of carloads of beer, now didn't have enough freight cars to meet war industry's need for transportation. The government now had a federal income tax which replaced the revenue tax on liquor. The saloonkeeper now ran a speakeasy, which operated undercover and therefore couldn't be legislated out of business by the women voters. Suddenly one gigantic power which had fought suffrage in the North and Midwest, and which had spent millions of dollars in elections to defeat woman suffrage amendments, was now only a deflated balloon.

Removed at the same time was the pressure on the National American, at the state and national level, to divert its energies to aiding the temperance movement. The Women's Christian Temperance Union and the Anti-Saloon League had raided the suffrage movement for workers and organizers. Many suffragettes had voluntarily devoted many hours to temperance work which otherwise could have strengthened the fight for the vote. But the W.C.T.U. and the Anti-Saloon League endorsed woman suffrage, and the Prohibition Party was the first to put a suffrage plank in its platform. Now these two organizations had nothing to fight but bootleggers.

The second great advantage to the suffrage cause, inadvertently perhaps handed to the women, was the fact that the Eighteenth Amendment temporarily punctured the states' rights bugaboo. The Eighteenth Amendment had its greatest support in the South and Southwest. Here were these ideological descendants of John C. Calhoun, Wade Hampton, Jefferson Davis, and John C. Breckinridge voting to permit the federal government to tell the people of their sovereign states that they couldn't drink liquor. Of course, many of them drank "wet" and voted "dry." But in voting for Prohibition they had muzzled themselves, if they were consistent, which some were not, against raising the states' rights cry against a woman suffrage amendment. Furthermore, the passage of the Eighteenth Amendment had weakened the alliance between the conservative Southern congressmen and the Northern representatives of the big city machines. The latter wanted the Eighteenth Amendment repealed with the end of the war.

Sensing the latter advantage, if not the first, Mrs. Catt set up permanent headquarters of her congressional committee in Washington, apart from the Association's building. Here was kept the voting record of every member of Congress. It was also used as a social center for political activity and public relations. When the D.A.R., the United Daughters of the Confederacy, the Sons of Union Veterans, garden clubs, PTA's, and Grangers visited Washington, they were invited to a tea or a reception at the headquarters of the congressional committee. Woman suffrage was not necessarily discussed, but from the heaps of literature on the tables, the charts on the walls, a list of equal rights states prominently posted, the visitors surely knew who they had to thank for the honors paid them.

As for the war effort — Mrs. Catt announced that the National American would sponsor a national contest for war posters: recruiting, Liberty Bonds, fuel conservation, war gardens, meatless days, Red Cross, European war relief, and general militant patriotism. Then she invited the winners to Washington and presented their originals in an art show in her headquarters. This drew public attention to the war services of the National American, and the show received wide publicity in the art columns of the metropolitan newspapers and monthly periodicals. The prizes were minuscule — totaling only $500 for the thirty winning posters.

Mrs. Catt's organization of the National American deeply impressed Secretary of War Newton D. Baker and impelled him to make this public statement to her: "We speak of this as a war for democracy. Women are making sacrifices just like men. If all the women were to stop their work tonight, we should have to withdraw from the war, at least temporarily, until we could entirely readjust ourselves. One of the things this war is bringing home to us is that men and women are essentially partners in an industrial civilization, and by the end of the war the women will be recognized as partners." And don't think that Carrie Chapman Catt lost any time in getting Secretary Baker's statement to the Associated Press, because it was reasonably certain that the statement would not have been made without President Wilson's approval.

But with all of her wartime activity, Mrs. Catt still found time to follow Susan Anthony's motto — AGITATE, EDUCATE, ORGANIZE. Mrs. Catt sent out a call for public demonstrations for what would now be the Nineteenth Amendment. Responding to her call, the suffragettes whooped it up in twenty-six states. Now, the women who marched and demonstrated were not just the girls from Vassar and Smith. They were women in coveralls, just off the night shift in the airplane factories, the women who worked the lathes to make gun barrels at the Colt factory in Hartford, Connecticut. They were the girls who loaded the cartridges and drove streetcars. Flush with funds, Mrs. Catt began buying advertising space in streetcars.

Now Mrs. Catt plunged into the political arena deeper than she had dared before. She issued a statement from headquarters, addressed to her state organizations, which now included Hawaii: "If the Sixty-fifth Congress fails to submit the Federal Amendment before the next congressional election [1918], this association shall select and enter into such a number of congressional campaigns as will effect a change in both Houses of Congress sufficient to insure its passage. The selection of candidates to be opposed is to be left to the Executive Board and to the boards of the states in question. Our opposition to individual candidates shall not be based on party considerations."

Strong stuff! Susan Anthony probably wouldn't have liked that command to Mrs. Catt's troops. Where Susan had petitioned, Carrie was threatening. There would be a blacklist and there would be those marked for political slaughter, regardless of party. In suffrage states such as Illinois, New York, and California, heads could fall.

In the spring of 1918, Mrs. Catt didn't even bother to appear at the hearings of the Senate Committee on Woman Suffrage. She sent representatives to the hearing which was only a formality. The committee was unanimous in its support of the proposed Nineteenth Amendment. The House was still to be heard from, but was dragging its feet.

During the summer of 1918, the activities of the National American Woman Suffrage Association were in limbo. The end of the war seemed to be in sight, but just when would it end? Congress was so buried in military legislation that it simply could not take the time for a lengthy debate over woman suffrage. In her threat to blacklist members of Congress who opposed the submission of a suffrage amendment, Mrs. Catt had warned that congressmen should not be marked for defeat should the situation in Europe deny Congress a chance for full consideration of the proposed Nineteenth Amendment. And this was just the situation in the congressional summer of 1918.

The deadline for calling a National American convention was November 1, and although Mrs. Catt could have no way of knowing that the war would end ten days after that, transportation problems the cost of living, the number of women in mourning, and the devotion of suffragists everywhere seemed to make a national convention entirely impossible. Then in November, the eleventh month, on the eleventh day, at the eleventh hour, the Armistice with Germany was declared, and for a few days no one, not even Carrie Chapman Catt, could think about woman suffrage.

But while Mrs. Catt had absolved Congress for not submitting a suffrage amendment to the state legislatures during 1918, they had nearly done it anyway. Surprisingly, it had been initiated in the House and passed by the requisite two-thirds majority, apparently without much debate. Perhaps Mrs. Catt's threat of heads to fall had been heeded. In the Senate, where Mrs. Catt believed that she had her most strength, the amendment lost by two votes. She was not pleased but at least satisfied — only two senators to convert or defeat in the next year. Victory was sure and at hand. In fact, she made the decision that massive political pressure was no longer necessary to force the submission of the Nineteenth Amendment. The days of the Militants were over, and so were the long hearings before the Houses of Congress. The greatest problem now was to prepare all the women of America for the vote. A strong believer in preparedness, Carrie Chapman Catt was already forgetting the National American Woman Suffrage Association and gradually constructing in her mind an organization which she had already named.

14   *The Last Roll Call*

The old-timers at the fiftieth and last active convention of
the National Woman Suffrage Association really didn't enjoy it very much. The crusade which they had begun in
1869 was over. There were at the convention delegates
from fifteen states where women had full suffrage. The last
attempt to put the proposed Nineteenth Amendment
through the Senate lost by only one vote. Obviously the
crusade was over. The prayers were too short, the older
delegates complained, and where were the long rousing
speeches of Susan Anthony's day? Yes, victory was just
around the corner, and for the veteran members of the
Association, the whole thing was an anticlimax.

The last national convention of the National American,
on its own, met in St. Louis, March 24, 1919. In her opening address, Mrs. Catt announced her plan for a new
organization, the League of Women Voters. The National
American would not dissolve until the Nineteenth Amendment was ratified. The League would recruit the women in
the fifteen states with full suffrage and promote voter-
education on local and national issues. The League of

Women Voters and the National American would work together in pressuring Congress.

Then Mrs. Catt outlined a program for the future which was certainly comprehensive and with goals hardly obtainable within a generation. It is interesting to note how many of these goals have been attained or have been found practical. They also point up the changes in serious political thinking over the past forty-seven years. Mrs. Catt's goals were: compulsory education, enforced by the federal government (we are a long way from that in the fullest sense); English the national language (impractical at present in New Mexico, Puerto Rican Harlem, and parts of Maine and New Hampshire); higher qualifications for citizenship (no change up to now); direct citizenship for women and not through marriage (achieved); compulsory lessons in citizenship through foreign language papers (compulsion is impractical in this case); oath of allegiance as qualification for citizenship (probably she meant naturalization); schools of citizenship in every ward and rural district (the former has been conducted mainly by the League of Women Voters, the public schools, and the American Legion; the trend toward educational requirements for voting is downward).

The next event at the convention was the dramatization of President Wilson's gradual reversal of his attitude on woman suffrage. On the platform a large parchment was unveiled, with the beautifully inscribed words of the President in his message to the Senate of September 30, 1918, asking the Senate to act on the Nineteenth Amendment.

The program was so crowded that only a general report for the year was read. Among the highlights were: (1) twenty-one Democratic and twenty Republican state conventions had endorsed the proposed Nineteenth Amendment; (2) Miss May Garrett Hay had been elected chairman of the Republican platform committee in New York and elected to the Republican National Committee; (3) in New Hampshire, where the suffragettes campaigned against Senator George H. Moses, he was nearly defeated, and in Delaware, where they attacked Senator Baird, he ran far behind the rest of his ticket.

Direct from the White House, the convention received President Wilson's unqualified support of the Nineteenth Amendment, and with this a move to change the wording of the Amendment, making it more acceptable to the South, was soundly defeated. Then the delegates departed, knowing that their last convention for any constructive work was completed. There would be another convention only for the purpose of liquidating the National American Woman Suffrage Association and to celebrate their victory. All they had to do in the next year was to change one Senate vote and hold the rest in line.

In May, 1919, Congress was in session, and the proceedings were unbearably dull. Legislation mainly concerned war claims for damages, alien property, government surplus, and the donating of captured cannon to decorate village greens, each congressman wanting a cannon for nearly every town in his district. To break the monotony, someone again introduced the proposed Nineteenth Amendment.

It would be much easier if this author could tell a story of blazing oratory, fiery debate, political intrigue, attempted bribery and fiibuster, but the elements of such a story just weren't there, and the reason was obvious. In May, 1919, women already had the vote in twenty-nine states controlling 306 electoral votes. There were men with presidential ambitions in both Houses of Congress.

On May 20, a resolution was introduced in the House referring the proposed Nineteenth Amendment to the Committee on Woman Suffrage. The only debate was over the composition of the committee, and it was purely partisan tactics. The Democrats objected to the referral, because House Speaker Gillette had not appointed the full complement of the Suffrage Committee, only Republicans. If the committee came out with a favorable report, the Republicans would get the credit. The Republicans controlled the House, and when the Amendment was passed, as it obviously would be by the Republican majority, the Democrats would have little about which to brag to the ladies when the presidential election came up in November.

But the Democratic members of the House could only fight a brief delaying action. Iron-fisted Frederick Gillette, Speaker of the House, ruled that since a majority of the committee had been appointed, it had a quorum and could function. The vote on the referral was 211 ayes — 12 nays.

Without even a hearing, and apparently with no discussion, the House Committee on Woman Suffrage was back the next morning with a favorable report. What followed could hardly be called a debate. Noses had been counted, but there was plenty of oratory. Nearly every congressman, regardless of his previous position and vote, was now clamoring for recognition to tell the nation how badly it needed woman suffrage, and what great things women's votes would do for the country. Although it was May, every representative had his eye on the November calendar.

Representative Edward C. Little (R) of Kansas led the procession of speakers: "Ninety-nine per cent of our murderers are men, ninety-nine per cent of the burglars are men. And the same goes for gamblers, forgers, counterfeiters, and *all* of the criminals. If good character were the basis for the franchise, most of the women would have been voters long ago. In the last analysis, those who oppose woman suffrage simply ignore everything but brute force."

Congressman Little's "Sunday punch" was; "the conquering armies camped on the Rhine have fought to establish the fact that civilization is better civilized than barbarism. If common sense is more potent than the sword, if men have determined on the field of battle that that is their intention and their law, then woman should have the same opportunity to take part in the life that men have always had."

Representative Frank Mondell, the lone congressman from Wyoming, the man from the pioneer suffrage state, concluded his speech: "We are proposing to invite the better half of mankind into participation in the settlement of the multiplied and multiplying situations of government, and we shall have better laws, better administration and a better world when that is accomplished."

The speeches in the House were many, but mercifully short, because before the end of the legislative day the roll call on the Nineteenth Amendment was an overwhelming 304 to 90 in the affirmative.

There was a slight delay in getting the Amendment into the Senate, the only obstruction being the opening debates on the League of Nations and the Versailles Treaty. A resolution for referring the proposed Nineteenth Amendment to the Senate Committee on Woman Suffrage came up on June 2, twelve days after the House victory. The resolution passed on a voice vote, and as happened in the House, the Senate Committee was back the next morning with a favorable report. The Senate nose count revealed the Amendment as a sure thing, but when the Senate took it up on June 3, it was soon obvious that a number of Antis were going to insist on being heard, and there were rumors of a Southern filibuster.

In order to give the Antis their say, and perhaps prevent the threatened filibuster, those in favor of the Amendment had little to say. They knew that the Nineteenth was in the bag. Thus, the debate which ensued was less over women voting than the Negro's civil rights and his franchise. The old legislative gimmick, "I question the presence of a quorum," was used again and again, each "question" requiring a roll call. Then a series of irrelevant amendments was offered by the opposition, each requiring a roll call.

The attitude of the opposition is probably best summed up in the speech of Senator Hardy of Texas, who said his state was considering a woman suffrage amendment and he hoped it would pass, but he revived the old and present argument, still heard in some places, that the United States should not interfere with the states' rights to establish voting qualifications even when they are established to exclude certain groups, races, creeds, or descendants of certain nationalities.

The majority of the Senate listened patiently for one long day. The filibuster didn't materialize, although a few Anti tonsils should have been sore by the end of the day. The Senate convened on June 4 and the final roll call was taken. The clerks of the Senate made a careful but hasty tally. They passed a sheet of paper to Vice President Thomas R. Marshall, presiding over the Senate, the man who said, "What this country needs is a good five-cent cigar."

The Vice President scanned the sheet carefully. Then he rapped with that little ivory knob which has no handle, and which Senate presidents have traditionally used, arose and announced, "The Yeas are sixty-six, the Nays thirty. A quorum being present, and the joint resolution having received the vote of more than two thirds of the senators present and voting, is declared to have passed the Senate in accordance with the Constitution of the United States."

Thomas Riley Marshall, Vice President of the United States, on June 3, 1919, announced the final tally of the Senate votes on the 19th Amendment: "The Yeas are sixty-six, the Nays thirty."

15   *The Impatient Interim*

The whole thing was an anticlimax. Everyone had known for months that woman suffrage was a shoo-in. If the women lit any bonfires on the night of June 4, no one ever wrote about them. There just wasn't any time for celebrating. The Nineteenth Amendment shot through Congress, but now it had to be ratified by two thirds of the states (38). There were fifteen months in which to get this accomplished, not an unreasonable period during the right circumstances. But the circumstances were all wrong.

In most states at the time, legislatures met biennially in the odd years. They were elected in November of the even years and convened sometime during the January of the odd year. Since state governments were not as complex as they are today, most legislatures were able to wind up their business by spring. Thus in July, 1919, there was probably not a legislature in the forty-eight states which was in session, and the majority of them would not reconvene until January, 1921, nearly three months after the presidential election.

There was only one solution to the problem, and it was a

long shot: to get enough governors to call special sessions of their legislatures to ratify the Amendment. Mrs. Chapman Catt certainly knew her arithmetic and her practical politics enough to recognize the odds she faced. In the first place, special sessions are very expensive. This would be an obstacle in any state whether for or against woman suffrage. They are unpopular with the legislators because they interfere with their personal occupations. There were nineteen states which had not granted suffrage to women up to that time. Would their governors be likely to call unpopular and expensive special sessions to vote for the Nineteenth Amendment and no other business? But these nineteen states represented one third of the forty-eight. If they didn't ratify, every other state would be needed if women were to vote in the 1920 presidential election.

There was another problem. In those states where women did not have the federal franchise, where they had voted, if at all, in school district and municipal elections, there was a tremendous voter-education need. Women must be informed on issues. They must know the election laws and know how to register and pass literacy tests.

This time, Carrie Chapman Catt unleashed her hardest-hitting campaign. First she appealed to the governors of the "easy" states where she hoped for cooperation. On the "tough" states, she turned to bluff and political blakmail. She bluffed them by telling them that the Nineteenth Amendment would be ratified by November, 1920, and those governors who refused to call special sessions of their legislatures, would be "remembered" on Election Day, and if by any stretch of the imagination, the women did not vote until 1922, those governors and their parties would be doubly "remembered." She also turned her guns on incumbent senators and told them that they should make every effort to influence their governors to call special sessions — or else.

The reaction to Mrs. Catt's strategy was immediate. Within six days after the Senate had voted — Illinois, Wisconsin, and Michigan had ratified. By June 28 Kansas, New York, Ohio, Pennsylvania (formerly Anti), Massachusetts, and most unlikely Texas had joined the ratification procession. Nine states in nineteen days! The early ratifications in Pennsylvania, Massachusetts, and Texas were wholly unexpected and caused Mrs. Catt to alter her tally sheet and timetable. Now she obtained the assent of the governors of Nebraska, Indiana, and Minnesota to write twenty-two other governors urging them to call special sessions.

Mrs. Catt then ran into the stumbling block which she had feared, the states which already had women suffrage. In the non-suffrage states, she had her organizations which could pressure the governor and the legislature. But in states where women already had suffrage, the women had affiliated with the party organizations of their choice and had dissolved their needless equal rights associations. Thus there was no group to exert political pressure on the state governments, and the governors were reluctant to call expensive special sessions of the legislatures to help the women in other states. Nevertheless, the ratifications marched on. By September 30, Iowa, Missouri, Arkansas, Montana, Nebraska, Minnesota, New Hampshire, and Utah had ratified, bringing the total number of ratifying states to seventeen — still far from the required thirty-eight, and with only two Far Western states on the roster.

Then there was a pause, and as always in a time of crisis Carrie Chapman Catt took to the road. Accompanied by a flying squadron of her best speakers and attorneys she held sixteen emergency conferences in twelve Western states during October. All but two of these states already had equal suffrage, but their governors had been reluctant to convene the legislatures.

As usual, Mrs. Catt got results when she went into action. The ratification drive immediately speeded up with North Dakota, Dec. 1; South Dakota, Dec. 4; Colorado, Dec. 12; Oregon, Jan. 12; and Nevada, Feb. 7.

While Mrs. Catt had been vigorously pressuring the governors in the Northwest, other states had ratified the Nineteenth Amendment with little need for organization on the part of the suffragettes. California and Maine had joined the list in November; Rhode Island, Kentucky, and Indiana in January. February brought another encouraging breakthrough in New Jersey, Idaho, Arizona, New Mexico, and Oklahoma. When Mrs. Catt totaled her tally sheet she found that thirty-two states had ratified. Only six more were needed, but when she checked the colored pins on her map, she noted the discouraging fact that only two states of the old Confederacy had ratified. There the going would be rough, and from the Old South she needed her six states, or so she thought. Her first move was characteristic of Catt strategy. She immediately raised a ratification fund of $100,000. Selecting Tennessee as her first target, Mrs. Catt charged into Nashville where she set up campaign headquarters. In the meantime she had received an assist from the opponents of woman suffrage throughout the nation and the United States Supreme Court, the latter removing the sting of *Minor versus Happersett.*

When the ratification resolution was before the Maine legislature, the Down East Antis had, through an Initiative and Referendum law, forced the legislature to submit ratification to the voters at large. Even though they lost in

Maine, the vote being in favor of ratification, the opponents of equal rights sought to make a last-ditch stand by applying the same technique in other states. The Ohio Supreme Court sustained a referendum petition, and the suffragettes appealed to the U.S. Supreme Court where the Ohio decision was overruled, the decision stating that the ratification of an amendment to the Federal Constitution was not subject to action by the voters. Governor Roberts of Tennessee had been waiting for the Supreme Court decision before calling a special session of the legislature.

This delay on the part of Governor Roberts by refusing to call a special session of the legislature until August 9 was agonizing to Carrie Chapman Catt, because events were happening outside Tennessee about which she could do little. Had she been able to foresee them with certainty, she never would have come to Nashville. While she was campaigning up and down Tennessee, enough states had ratified the Nineteenth Amendment to leave the final outcome in the hands of the Tennessee legislature. If Tennessee should fail to ratify, and the vote was in doubt, the women of the forty-eight states would not vote in the 1920 presidential election.

Now Carrie Chapman Catt faced the most crucial hour in her more than twenty years as the American leader in the crusade for woman suffrage. She had generaled an army of two million women through years of battles in Congress and the state legislatures. Up to now she had eventually won every battle, in the school districts, municipal elections, in twenty-nine state legislatures, in the House and Senate, and in the ratification of the Nineteenth Amendment by thirty-seven states. Now she had to win one more state, and in a legislature which had not displayed any enthusiasm for equal rights, or end her career in defeat. She could feel the spirits of Lucretia Mott, Elizabeth Cady Stanton, Susan B. Anthony, and Lucy Stone standing before her saying in a chorus, "You just can't let us down."

Mrs. Catt realized that her army of two million women couldn't help her in Tennessee. She didn't have enough Tennessee women to organize a parade. If she brought in a trainload of Militants, they would get themselves arrested and her chances of victory in the Tennessee legislature would vanish. She couldn't even find much to do effectively with the $100,000 she had raised. There was only one alternative — "Shoot the works," and she wheeled up the heaviest pieces of political artillery she had ever mustered.

The presidential election was only two months and a few days away. The women of America might decide the outcome if the Nineteenth Amendment became part of the Constitution before Election Day. The Democrats and Republicans were both fearful of, and hoping for the woman vote. They both remembered, especially the Democrats, the short shrift they had given the women at their national conventions. Senator Wadsworth of New York remembered his wife's violent attacks on woman suffrage. It is certain that Republican candidate Warren G. Harding had only to look in the mirror to convince himself that he was physically more attractive than the Democrat Cox; and incumbent, ailing President Wilson had already gone all out for the Nineteenth Amendment. All except Wilson had been campaigning since June, and they were leaving no electoral stone unturned.

With her unerring political know-how, Carrie Catt nearly equaled Lyndon Baines Johnson in making the most of a situation. Telegrams calling for help went out to candidates

Warren Gamaliel Harding, who successfully ran
against James Cox in 1920, the year of victory for
woman's suffrage with the passage of the 19th
Amendment.

Harding and Cox, to the White House, to the chairmen of
the Democratic and Republican national committees, to
numerous state party committee chairmen, and to such
respected U.S. Senators as Ashurst of Arizona, Walsh of
Massachusetts, and La Follette of Wisconsin.

Now, the telegrams and letters were pouring back into
Nashville addressed to Governor Roberts, and the majority
and minority leaders of the Tennessee House and Senate.
The chairman of the Tennessee Democratic State Committee got his share of pressure from his national chairman
in Washington. The Republican leaders in the Northeast

counties of the state soon knew how Republican National Committee chairman Will Hays felt about the Nineteenth Amendment. Then came the statements from Warren G. Harding, Calvin Coolidge, James M. Cox, and Franklin D. Roosevelt.

Governor Roberts immediately realized that Mrs. Chapman Catt had whipped up a bipartisan storm. As a Southern Democrat he simply couldn't buck the Wilson-Cox-Roosevelt pressure. The national political pressure on the Tennessee Senate was effective, and the ratification resolution passed by a safe margin on September 13, but in the House, it was immediately in trouble. The House debated the resolution for five days. Then it squeaked through, but that wasn't the final victory. The opponents of the resolution demanded a vote for reconsideration which was parliamentarily in order.

What happened at this point — whether or not Mrs. Catt was responsible for it — this author has been unable to determine. But when the vote to reconsider was called for, enough supporters of the Nineteenth Amendment in the Tennessee House of Representatives were absent to prevent a quorum. The sergeant-at-arms of the House was sent to round them up with the threat of a "Contempt of the House" charge, but they couldn't be found. Their kinfolk said that they had suddenly been called away on business — business outside Tennessee. It is pure speculation, but the author has the notion that Carrie Catt knew where they were.

By August 24, there still not being a quorum in the Tennessee House to vote on reconsideration of the ratification resolution, Governor Roberts forwarded a certificate of ratification to Wilson's Secretary of State, Bainbridge Colby. In Washington, on August 26, 1920, Secretary of

State Colby proclaimed the Nineteenth Amendment part of the Federal Constitution. Somewhere, those brave ladies Mott, Stanton, Anthony, and Stone must have said, "Well done, Carrie." And probably somewhere else, a couple of New England clergymen said, "Why didn't we have better sense than to drive Lucretia Mott and Elizabeth Stanton out of the London Anti-Slavery Convention back in 1840?"

That night in 1920, Carrie Chapman Catt said, "The vote is won. For seventy-two years the battle for this privilege has been waged, but human affairs with their eternal change move on without pause. Progress is calling on you to make no pause. Act!"

16   *After the Victory*

November 2, 1920, was a beautiful, warm, sunny day. In the Democratic South, the oak leaves were turning a golden brown, and in Republican New England, the trees were bare, permitting the autumn sun to pour down on the white town halls where the polls had just opened. In front of the polling places were parked Model-T Fords, Maxwells, Overlands, and a few new Buicks with natural-finish, wooden wheels. The cars, in a day before bumper stickers, were covered with hand-painted signs: KEEP THE WORLD SAFE FOR DEMOCRACY . . . BACK TO NORMALCY WITH HARDING . . . VOTE FOR HARD-ING AND COOLIDGE . . . VOTE FOR COX AND ROOSEVELT.

In front of the Town Hall, a group of local politicians were basking in the November sun, checking off the members of their parties who entered the polls. One of them said to the group "When d'ye expect the first one will show up?" The chairman of the Republican town committee replied, "Well, I know one who won't. Ernie Hadlock told his wife this mornin', 'Tuesday's ironin' day, so you jest stay home and git my shirts done.' So that's one vote the Democrats won't git."

And then the big moment came. A surrey with fringe on top pulled up directly in front of the Town Hall, and down stepped a tall, slender, very erect woman with a high lace collar and pince-nez glasses. She was the Regent of the local D.A.R. However, she had been an avid suffragette, was a devotee of murder mysteries, and would later lecture her D.A.R. chapter on why Mae West was her favorite actress. When she entered the Town Hall and approached the supervisors of the check list, they removed their hats and dropped their cigar butts into the convenient spittoon. The chairman of the Republican town committee said to a colleague, "Well, we got the first one."

By mid-afternoon, when the voting in both parties was slow, the local political satraps awoke to the fact that they had a "woman vote" to bring in. The town committeemen checked their lists and the number of women who had voted, which included the Regent of the D.A.R., the wives of the superintendent of schools, the Congregational minister, the candidates for the legislature, and a former member of the Smith College Marching Suffragettes.

Then the Model T's, Hudsons, Stanley Steamers, and a lone Pierce-Arrow began to roll. But they came back with few women. Stopping at house after house, offering transportation to the polls, they got the same answers: "Oh, my husband wouldn't like it" . . . "I'd have to change my dress" . . . "I've got red flannel hash on the stove, and I can't leave it" . . . "You see, I'm for Cox, and my husband is for Harding, so we'd just cancel out."

Considering how long the Nineteenth Amendment had been stalled in the Tennessee legislature, and the lack of time to get women registered by November 2, the registra-

Women voting for the first time.

tion drive proved to have been just short of miraculous. How many women voted throughout the country, of course, cannot be known, but a comparison of the election statistics of 1920 with those of 1916 shows that something happened — there just weren't that many more men in 1920. In 1916, the combined vote for Wilson and Hughes was 16,667,827; the combined vote for Harding and Cox was 25,299,556, an increase of 8,631,729!

It is anyone's guess how the women voted in the 1920 election, but it is obvious that they helped to swell Harding's majority. Had Wilson been a well man, the outcome might have been different to some degree. Wilson's program for world peace through the League of Nations should have been attractive to women. But Wilson, ill and paralyzed,

Men (background) smile as mothers and wives line up to enroll their names on the voting register. Many had predicted that few women would exercise their new rights.

Men play nurse at polls in Chicago while women cast their vote.

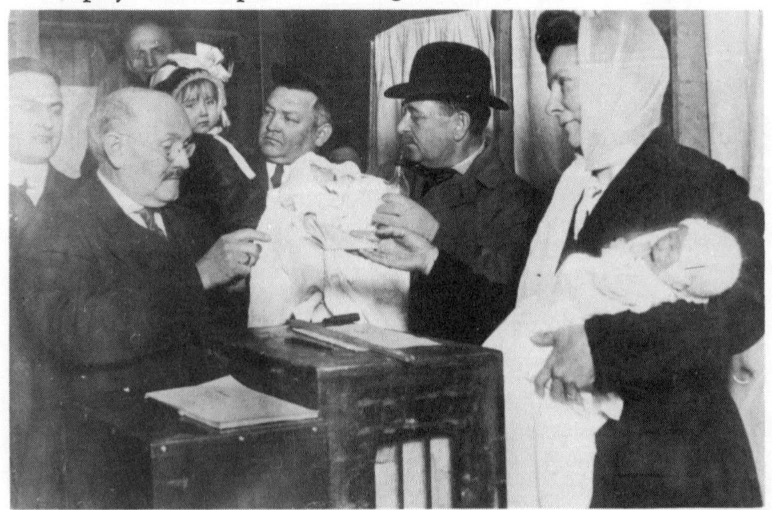

was unble to campaign for Cox. The League had been so castigated in the Senate that neither Cox nor his running mate, Franklin Roosevelt, made much of the issue during the campaign. No one knew where Harding stood on any issue except that he was for "back to normalcy," and after wartime food shortages, high prices, and "meatless days," that slogan probably appealed to women.

There is one organization which perhaps can be given credit for the short-notice participation in the 1920 election, the institution which superseded the National American Woman Suffrage Association — the League of Women Voters of the United States.

In 1920, in anticipation of the ratification of the Nineteenth Amendment, Carrie Chapman Catt dissolved the National American and passed the torch to the League of Women Voters which she conceived as the organization to organize and educate women voters after her job was done. Expecting that it would take time for the major parties to recognize the value of integrating the women into their organizations, Mrs. Catt said: "If we are going to trail behind the Democrats and Republicans about five years, and if our program is going to be that much behind the dominant political parties, we might as well quit before we begin. If the League of Women Voters hasn't the vision to see what is coming, and be five years ahead of the political parties, I doubt if it is worth the trouble to go on."

In this statement, Mrs. Catt displayed her innate political know-how, although she underestimated the city machines and the top echelons of the two major parties in recognizing the potential of the "woman vote." The city machines didn't want the former suffragette. They would wait until they could develop female leaders among the ethnic groups of their parties: Jews, Negroes, Poles,

Italians, Swedes, and Slovaks. After they had developed them, they sometimes wished that they had taken in the suffragettes, for they found themselves with the true reformers — the women who knew about blocked fire escapes, cold-water flats, inadequate garbage collection, and lack of recreational areas. These women would eventually bolt their Tammany bosses and elect "The Little Flower," Fiorello H. La Guardia.

But Mrs. Catt completely underestimated the speed with which women interested in politics would be absorbed and given positions of responsibility in the two major parties outside the large cities. Almost immediately, they were serving on town, county and state committees. Where they used to sing "Getting the Ballot for the Mothers," they were now writing and singing songs for Republican and Democratic rallies. They were registering women who had not been able to get to the polls in 1920, and they used their husbands' cars to drive voters to the polls in the 1922 biennial election.

Some prominent women were disappointed in the female reaction to suffrage. They had envisioned a "woman vote." They had naively expected that women, although registering as Democrats or Republicans, would unite as a sex on certain issues and vote for them, regardless of party affiliation. Among these women was Mrs. Alice Roosevelt Longworth, daughter of Theodore Roosevelt and wife of "Nick" Longworth, Republican Speaker of the House. After the 1920 election, she wondered "if it had been worth it all."

There was no "woman vote" in 1920, and there probably never will be one. Women are individuals just like men. There is no reason to believe that they will ever unite on a single issue any more than men do — except on the support of a nonpartisan issue involving the security of the United States. Most of them will join with their husbands and congressmen in backing the President. But on such issues as foreign aid, the admission of Red China to the UN, or crop price supports, the women will never agree as a voting bloc.

Carrie Chapman Catt foresaw that women would be Republicans, Democrats, or independents. This she encouraged, but she insisted that these women in their three categories *be informed*. She abhorred blind partisan voting without knowledge. She saw the role of the League of Women Voters as nonpartisan, giving both parties the opportunity to explain their position, placing these opposing attitudes on record, and then presenting them without bias to the members of the League.

Now came the question: What, besides voting and participating in party organizations, would be woman's role in government? Jeanette Rankin of Montana was already a veteran of the House of Representatives, but she had not enhanced the popular image of women in politics by having been the only member of Congress to vote against the declaration of war on Germany in 1917. This had led to the charge from the wife of Senator Wadsworth of New York that the whole woman suffrage movement was pro-German.

Would governors and Presidents appoint women to positions of responsibility without discrimination? Would there ever be a woman governor of a state, a senator, or even might there be, within the next generation, a woman candidate for President, nominated by a major party, and without the shenanigans of Victoria Woodhull?

The answers were not long in coming as compared with the eighty-year struggle for the vote. In the 1920's a year's

Appointed Assistant Attorney General by President Harding, Mabel Walker Willebrandt led the way for other women into responsible government positions.

progress represented decades in the days of Susan Anthony and Lucy Stone. Soon after moving into the White House, President Warren G. Harding appointed Mabel Walker Willebrandt to the post of Assistant Attorney General.

Mrs. Willebrandt had been born in Woodsdale, Kansas,

in 1889. While a schoolteacher in Pasadena, California, she married A. F. Willebrandt in 1910. After studying law, she was appointed public defender of women in the Los Angeles County courts. There she defended more than 2,000 women charged with shoplifting, prostitution, possession of narcotics, and other common violations, who could not afford legal counsel. In Washington, she was placed in charge of Prohibition enforcement, tax laws and the Bureau of Federal Prisons. She remained with the Department of Justice until 1929, when she resigned to head a company that made bricks of compressed grapes combined with chemicals which would produce wine when soaked in water. Mrs. Willebrandt had learned a lot about the Prohibition laws while Assistant U.S. Attorney General.

The women were apparently as bored as the men with the 1924 presidential election. The combined vote for Calvin Coolidge, Republican, and John W. Davis, Democrat, was one million less than that of 1920. The country was prosperous (on paper), and the Republican slogan "Keep Cool with Coolidge" prevailed. However, on August 23, preceding the presidential election, Mrs. Miriam A. Ferguson, known as "Ma" Ferguson, won the Democratic nomination for governor of Texas, assuring her election.

To call "Ma" Ferguson the first woman governor in the United States is factual but beclouds the circumstances under which she arrived, or more accurately stayed in the governor's mansion. In most Southern states, a governor cannot succeed himself immediately. "Pa" Ferguson had been governor of Texas for four years and, barred from running for re-election, he ran his wife to serve as a "chair warmer" for the next four years, after which he could run again. The first woman to be elected governor of a state on her own merits was Nellie Taylor Ross of Wyoming.

Muriel A. ("Ma") Ferguson of Texas became the first woman governor of a sovereign state.

After "Ma" Ferguson's election in Texas, there were occasions when the death of a U.S. senator came in an "off year," and the governor of the state would appoint the widow to serve until the next general election. In some cases, as in Arkansas, Hattie Caraway was appointed to succeed her husband, and then was elected in her own right. A recent example is U.S. Senator Maureen Neuberger of Oregon.

Widow of U.S. Senator Richard Neuberger, Maurine Neuberger of Oregon ran for and won her late husband's seat.

But by the 1930's, women were running for high public offices with the support of their party organizations. In 1928, Mrs. Ruth Baker Pratt (R) was elected to Congress from New York's 17th Congressional District. Nellie Taylor Ross (D) was elected Governor of Wyoming, and was later appointed Director of the U.S. Mint by President Franklin D. Roosevelt. At the same time, 1933, he appointed Frances Perkins Secretary of Labor, the first woman member of the Cabinet. In the last Congress, there were two women

The nation's second lady governor, Nellie Taylor Ross of Wyoming, who later was appointed Director of the Bureau of the Mint.

senators and eight representatives.

In January, 1964, Senator Margaret Chase Smith of Maine announced her candidacy for the Republican presidential nomination by entering her name in the New Hampshire (first in the nation) presidential primary. If any political historian scratched his head and said, "Is this going to be another Victoria Woodhull campaign?" he didn't know Margaret Chase Smith or her political record. And if he had checked her governmental experience against those of

Maine's spirited Margaret Chase Smith has served for 18 years in the
U.S. Senate. In 1964 she campaigned for the Republican presidential
nomination, the first woman candidate since Victoria Woodhull.

Governor Rockefeller, Henry Cabot Lodge, or Senator Goldwater, he would have had to admit that Senator Smith topped the field in that respect.

The first woman to seek the Presidency since Victoria Woodhull was elected to the House of Representatives in 1940 to fill the vacancy created by her husband's death. Her first congressional assignment was to the Naval Affairs Committee. In 1948, she was elected to the Senate by the greatest total vote majority in the history of Maine. In 1960, she was re-elected to her third Senate term, again the record vote-getter.

In the Senate by 1964, she had served on the Space Committee, the powerful Appropriations Committee, and the Armed Services Committee. As to her military record, she outranks former President Truman by having been a lieutenant colonel in the Air Force Reserve.

Why did Margaret Chase Smith, no militant feminist, decide to run for the Republican presidential nomination? She gave her reasons in a speech before the Women's National Press Club in Washington, D.C., on January 27, 1964. First, she recounted the reasons why she should not run, according to some of her friends in Washington.

"First, there are those who contend that no woman should ever aspire to the White House — that this is a man's world and that it should be kept that way.

"Second, it is contended that as a woman I would not have the physical stamina to run — that I should not take that much out of me for what might conceivably be a good cause, even if a losing one.

"Third, it is contended that I should not run because obviously I do not have the financial resources that the others have.

"Fourth, it is contended that I should not run because I

do not have the professional political organization that others have.

"Fifth, it is contended that I should not run because to do so would result in necessary absence from Washington while the Senate had roll-call votes — and thus I would bring to an end my consecutive roll-call record which is now at 1,590."

Senator Smith now said, "So because of these very impelling reasons against my running, I have decided that I shall — enter the New Hampshire primary. For I accept the reasons against my running as challenges. . . . My candidacy in the New Hampshire primary will be a test in several ways:

"(1) It will test how much support will be given a candidate without campaign funds . . . and whose whole expense will be paid by the candidate.

"(2) It will test how much support will be given a candidate without a professional organization of paid campaign workers but instead composed of amateur volunteers.

"(3) It will test how much support will be given a candidate who refuses to absent herself from the duties to which she was elected and whose campaign time in New Hampshire will be limited to those times when the Senate is not in session voting on legislation.

"I welcome the challenge and look forward to the test."

This author had the opportunity to observe the New Hampshire campaign of Senator Smith and compare it with those of Barry Goldwater and Nelson Rockefeller. Of course, Henry Cabot Lodge, who was in Vietnam, did not come into the state, although he carried it.

Anyone who said that Senator Smith lacked the necessary physical strength should have seen her in action. Driving her own inexpensive car, she visited every city and hamlet in the state. She shook hands in every supermarket and general store. One morning at 7 A.M. she drove up a mountain to the tiny town of Ellsworth with fourteen registered voters. There is no village center in Ellsworth and no store, only widely scattered farms. But by 8 A.M. every one of the fourteen voters had shaken Senator Smith's hand. She had nary a bumper sticker, pin, or newspaper ad. In some towns she had volunteers to introduce her to townspeople on the street, in others she had to go it alone.

It is impossible to assess the results of Senator Smith's New Hampshire campaign. The presidential primary is so complex in itself, and the voting conditions on that Town Meeting Day were so abnormal that the result was a complete enigma. The voters averaged from ten to twenty minutes in the voting booths, because they had entered with fistfuls of ballots: the ballot for town offices, another for delegates to the constitutional convention, a referendum ballot on the proposed New Hampshire Sweepstakes, and two presidential primary ballots.

One primary ballot contains the names of candidates for delegate to the party's national convention. The other ballot, which legally counts for nothing, is for the voter to express who he or she wants to be the party's presidential candidate, regardless of who the delegates are. In New Hampshire, this ballot is known as "the beauty contest."

Since Senator Smith had no candidates for delegate, her name appeared only in the "beauty contest." In the "wackiest" of New Hampshire presidential primaries, Henry Cabot Lodge, who was in South Vietnam and had never been in New Hampshire on a political mission, topped the field with 33,007 votes in the "beauty contest." Goldwater followed with 20,692. Margaret Chase Smith received 2,120. However, that number of Republicans preferred her over Harold Stassen (1,373) and Governor Scranton of Pennsylvania (105). Thus, there were 2,120 who would go along with having a woman President.

17 Today's Woman Voter

What is the American woman voter of today? Of course, there is no answer to such a question. A lifetime of political research could not produce such a creature any more than it could analyze the typical male voter. Perhaps better than research is experience, although there are limitations to both.

Remembering that there is no such person as *the woman voter,* let us measure her against what the opponents of woman suffrage said she would be, and what the supporters of the movement said she would do to improve the political scene.

The Antis said that her place was in the home, and that voting would take her away from her duties as a mother. However, even in the most rural areas, it seldom takes a woman more than forty-five minutes to drive to the polls, to vote and return. Most mothers bring their preschool children to the polls with them. There is always a candidate present only too eager to bounce the child on his knee while Mother is in the voting booth. Furthermore, it is a common practice today for political parties to provide baby-sitters as well as transportation. While there are women, political "pros," who devote a great deal of time to working at party headquarters, this is no different from millions of working mothers also away from home.

A charge of the Anti was that women would be debased by going to the polling places, and the counter-claim was that they would clean them up. The overwhelming evidence is for the latter. Whether it is a fire station, a town hall, a school auditorium or a vacant store, the polling place has certainly become more of a temple of democracy than it was in 1900. The woman not only votes there, but most often women are in charge of the registration lists and serve as ballot clerks where paper ballots are still used. It may be pure coincidence, but chewing tobacco went out of style at about the same time as the ratification of the Nineteenth Amendment.

The opposition charged that women would be more influenced by their emotions than men in voting. This may be true *to a slight extent*. But the term *emotion* must be tempered with *independence*. There are nearly as many hard-core, party-line women voters as men. They vote the straight ticket regardless of who is on the ballot. Their numbers are diminishing in both sexes. But there are more women than men who will "jump the fence," either because of principle or emotion, and this reaches right up to the top level of state party organizations.

In the final assessment, nobody knows what the voter, male or female, does behind the curtain of the voting booth or the voting machine, but something can be garnered from registration records. Although both men and women are less inclined to vote a straight ticket than they were thirty years ago, women no longer hesitate, as they did in 1920, to register in a party rivaling that of their husbands.

Many Democratic "pros" are wives of Republicans.

In regard to the fears of the city machines that women would upset the applecart, these applecarts have been upset only by independent male and female voters.

In most of the functions required by a political organization, women make better workers than men. One of the most important tasks of a political party is voter registration, and here the woman has a distinct advantage. When she goes out ringing doorbells, door to door, the housewife usually invites her in. She may even be offered a cup of coffee and time to talk about the candidate for whom she is campaigning, as well as time to convince the housewife that it is her duty to register and vote.

Women are more amenable to political training than men. In order to conduct modern political campaigns the worker must know how to build mailing lists and card files, registration techniques, fund raising, scheduling of candidates, publicity, organizing transportation for Election Day, mailing and telephone committees, radio scripts, bumper sticker distribution, organizing baby-sitters.

While men raise or give the largest donations to campaign funds, the huge cost of today's campaigns requires the raising of additional sums in small contributions. Over the past six years, Dollars-for-Democrats has been staffed almost entirely by women.

Some politicians have charged that the physical attractiveness of a male candidate influences the "woman vote," but this charge could hardly be validated by the victories of Calvin Coolidge, Herbert Hoover, Harry Truman, or Lyndon Johnson; nor can it be justified by the defeats of Thomas E. Dewey and Wendell Willkie, nor by the very narrow margin of victory for John F. Kennedy.

Do woman voters tend to unite on moral issues? First, it is difficult to define a moral issue. Was the repeal of

Prohibition a moral issue? If so, women certainly did not unite against it, since the vote in many states would indicate that women voted overwhelmingly to erase the Eighteenth Amendment from the Constitution. Was the creation of the New Hampshire Sweepstakes a moral issue? Most of the Protestant clergy in the state thought it was but the vote in its favor at the March referendum indicated that a large percentage of New Hampshire women did not agree.

The League of Women Voters at first attempted to make its influence felt on the platform committees of the two major parties. In 1919, when the League replaced the old National American, it came out in favor of the League of Nations. Then it found that it had a hot potato and dropped the issue. Since then, the League has supported Social Security, broadening of Civil Service coverage, the Food Drug and Cosmetic Act of 1938, Lend-Lease during World War II, the United Nations, Atomic Energy Control, and NATO. How much the League influences the votes of its members is unknown even by its officers. But when the League takes a position, it sees to it that its members are fully aware of the arguments, pro and con, on the subject.

Young women today are making important contributions to the Young Democratic and the Young Republican clubs. They work at party headquarters on mailings, help at rallies, staff the polls on Election Day, learning political techniques and informing themselves of their party's principles in order to become intelligent voters. Some of this work sounds like drudgery, but there are compensations — the excitement of working with people making the headlines. At Kennedy headquarters in Manchester just before the Presidential primary of 1960, a team of teen-age girls was helping to address and stuff 75,000 mailings. Sitting at the same long table, shoulder to shoulder with them, also stuffing and addressing, were Robert F. Kennedy, Ted Kennedy, Larry O'Brien, and Ted Sorensen.

Yes, since St. Paul issued his edict: "Women shall keep silence. . . ." theologians have pondered this edict. Politicians, too, have wondered about the woman in politics. They realize that their party machinery would collapse without the ladies. They need their help to get the vote out. But when a woman goes behind the curtain in the polling place, the politicians have no way of knowing what she will do.

To get back to Susan B. Anthony's observation and to bring it up to date: although electricity is much less an unknown quantity than it was when Miss Susan made her statement, the individual woman voter is still largely an unknown quantity. Her influence cannot be measured — only evaluated as being sufficiently precious — to be wooed and won.

Bibliography

Adams, James Truslow: *The March of Democracy*, Charles Scribner's Sons, New York, 1932.

Bancroft, Hubert Howe: *History of Nevada, Colorado and Wyoming*, The History Company Publishers, San Francisco, 1890.

: *History of Utah, 1540-1886*, The History Co., San Francisco, 1889.

Blackwell, Alice Stone: *Lucy Stone, Pioneer of Woman's Rights*, Little, Brown, Boston, 1930.

Buckmaster, Henrietta: *Let My People Go*, Harper & Brothers, New York, 1941.

Cheney, Ednah D.: *Louisa May Alcott, Her Life, Letters and Journals*, Little, Brown, Boston, 1928.

Elliot, Maude Howe: *Three Generations*, Little, Brown, Boston, 1923.

Evans, Lawrence B.: *Leading Cases on American Constitutional Law*, Callaghan, Chicago, 1925.

Finley, Ruth E.: *The Lady of Godey's, Sarah Josepha Hale*, Lippincott, Philadelphia, 1931.

Foster, G.A.: *The Eyes and Ears of the Civil War*, Criterion Books, New York, 1963.

League of Women Voters: *Forty Years of a Great Idea*, Washington, D.C., 1960.

Longworth, Alice Roosevelt: *Crowded Hours*, Charles Scribner's Sons, New York, 1933.

Maitland, Frederic W., and Montague, Francis: *A Sketch of English Legal History*, G.P. Putnam's Sons, New York, 1915.

Mill, John Stuart: *The Subjection of Women*, National American Woman Suffrage Association, New York, 1895.

Nevins, Allan: *The Emergence of Modern America*, 1865-1878, The Macmillan Company, New York, 1927.

New Hampshire, State of: *Justice and Sheriff*, G. Parker Lyon, Concord, 1843.

Oberholtzer, Ellis Paxson: *A History of the United States Since The Civil War* (6 vols.), Macmillan, New York, 1928.

Perley: Moore, E. Ben: *Perley's Reminiscences* (2 vols.), Hubbard Brothers, Philadelphia, 1886.

Pringle, Henry F.: *The Life and Times of William Howard Taft*, Farrar & Rinehart, New York, 1939.

Sachs, Emanie: *The Terrible Siren*: *Victoria Woodhull*, 1838-1927, Harper and Brothers, New York, 1928.

Stanton, Elizabeth Cady; Anthony, Susan B.; and many others: *History of Woman Suffrage*, (5 vols.), Fowler & Wells, New York, 1881-1920.

Stegner, Wallace, edited by Erskine Caldwell: *Mormon Country*, Duell, Sloane & Pearce, New York, 1942.

Stowe, Harriet Beecher: *The Key to Uncle Tom's Cabin*, Jewett, Proctor & Worthington, Boston, 1852.

Sullivan, Mark: *Our Times — The Turn of the Century*, Charles Scribner's Sons, New York, 1926.

Tharp, Louise Hall: *The Peabody Sisters of Salem*, Little, Brown, Boston, 1950.

U.S. Senate and House of Representatives: *Congressional Record*, 1919, U.S. Government Printing Office, Washington, D.C., 1919.